LAW, CRIME AND LAW ENFORCEMENT

INMATE RELEASE, REINTEGRATION AND REENTRY

ELEMENTS AND ANALYSIS

LAW, CRIME AND LAW ENFORCEMENT

Additional books in this series can be found on Nova's website under the Series tab.

Additional E-books in this series can be found on Nova's website under the E-book tab.

LAW, CRIME AND LAW ENFORCEMENT

INMATE RELEASE, REINTEGRATION AND REENTRY

ELEMENTS AND ANALYSIS

CHRIS HOMESLEY
EDITOR

New York

For permission to use material from this book please contact us:
Telephone 631-231-7269; Fax 631-231-8175
Web Site: http://www.novapublishers.com

Additional color graphics may be available in the e-book version of this book.

Library of Congress Cataloging-in-Publication Data

ISBN: 978-1-62417-996-9

Published by Nova Science Publishers, Inc. † New York

CONTENTS

PREFACE

The prison population in the United States has been growing steadily for more than 30 years. The Bureau of Justice Statistics reports that since 2000 an average of 680,000 inmates have been released from state and federal prisons and almost 5 million ex-offenders are under some form of community-based supervision. Offender reentry can include all the activities and programming conducted to prepare ex-convicts to return safely to the community and to live as law-abiding citizens. Some ex-offenders, however, eventually end up back in prison. This book examines the key elements in inmate release and offender reentry, with a focus on correctional statistics, reintegration into the community, and recidivism.

Chapter 1 – The prison population in the United States has been growing steadily for more than 30 years. The Bureau of Justice Statistics reports that since 2000 an average of 680,000 inmates have been released from state and federal prisons and almost 5 million ex-offenders are under some form of community-based supervision. Offender reentry can include all the activities and programming conducted to prepare ex-convicts to return safely to the community and to live as law-abiding citizens. Some ex-offenders, however, eventually end up back in prison. The most recent national-level recidivism study is 10 years old; this study showed that two-thirds of ex-offenders released in 1994 came back into contact with the criminal justice system within three years of their release. Compared with the average American, ex-offenders are less educated, less likely to be gainfully employed, and more likely to have a history of mental illness or substance abuse—all of which have been shown to be incarceration risk factors.

Three phases are associated with offender reentry programs: programs that take place during incarceration, which aim to prepare offenders for their eventual release; programs that take place during offenders' release period, which seek to connect ex-offenders with the various services they may require; and long-term programs that take place as ex-offenders permanently reintegrate into their communities, which attempt to provide offenders with support and supervision. There is a wide array of offender reentry program designs, and these programs can differ significantly in range, scope, and methodology. Researchers in the offender reentry field have suggested that the best programs begin during incarceration and extend throughout the release and reintegration process. Despite the relative lack of research in the field of offender reentry, an emerging "what works" literature suggests that programs focusing on work training and placement, drug and mental health treatment, and housing assistance have proven to be effective.

The federal government's involvement in offender reentry programs typically occurs through grant funding, which is available through a wide array of federal programs at the Departments of Justice, Labor, Education, and Health and Human Services. However, only a handful of grant programs in the federal government are designed explicitly for offender reentry purposes.

The Second Chance Act (P.L. 110-199) was enacted on April 9, 2008. The act expanded the existing offender reentry grant program at the Department of Justice and created a wide array of targeted grant-funded pilot programs.

Chapter 2 – About 700,000 inmates are released from federal and state custody each year, and another 9 million are booked into and released from local jails. Former inmates face challenges as they transition into, or reenter, society, such as finding housing and employment. According to the most recent data available, more than two-thirds of state prisoners are rearrested for a new offense within 3 years of release, and about half are reincarcerated. Federal reentry grants are available for state and local providers, as successful reentry reduces rearrest or reincarceration, known as recidivism. GAO was asked to review (1) the extent to which there is fragmentation, overlap, and duplication across federal reentry grant programs; (2) the coordination efforts federal grant-making agencies have taken to prevent unnecessary duplication and share promising practices; and (3) the extent to which federal grant-making agencies measure grantees' effectiveness in reducing recidivism. GAO identified and analyzed the grant programs and agencies that supported reentry efforts in fiscal year 2011; analyzed agency documents, such as grant solicitations; and interviewed agency officials.

In: Inmate Release, Reintegration and Reentry ISBN: 978-1-62417-996-9
Editor: Chris Homesley

Chapter 1

OFFENDER REENTRY: CORRECTIONAL STATISTICS, REINTEGRATION INTO THE COMMUNITY, AND RECIDIVISM*

Nathan James

SUMMARY

The prison population in the United States has been growing steadily for more than 30 years. The Bureau of Justice Statistics reports that since 2000 an average of 680,000 inmates have been released from state and federal prisons and almost 5 million ex-offenders are under some form of community-based supervision. Offender reentry can include all the activities and programming conducted to prepare ex-convicts to return safely to the community and to live as law-abiding citizens. Some ex-offenders, however, eventually end up back in prison. The most recent national-level recidivism study is 10 years old; this study showed that two-thirds of ex-offenders released in 1994 came back into contact with the criminal justice system within three years of their release. Compared with the average American, ex-offenders are less educated, less likely to be gainfully employed, and more likely to have a history of mental illness or substance abuse—all of which have been shown to be incarceration risk factors.

---

* This is an edited, reformatted and augmented version of a Congressional Research Service publication, CRS Report for Congress RL34287, from www.crs.gov, prepared for Members and Committees of Congress, dated December 7, 2011.

Three phases are associated with offender reentry programs: programs that take place during incarceration, which aim to prepare offenders for their eventual release; programs that take place during offenders' release period, which seek to connect ex-offenders with the various services they may require; and long-term programs that take place as ex-offenders permanently reintegrate into their communities, which attempt to provide offenders with support and supervision. There is a wide array of offender reentry program designs, and these programs can differ significantly in range, scope, and methodology. Researchers in the offender reentry field have suggested that the best programs begin during incarceration and extend throughout the release and reintegration process. Despite the relative lack of research in the field of offender reentry, an emerging "what works" literature suggests that programs focusing on work training and placement, drug and mental health treatment, and housing assistance have proven to be effective.

The federal government's involvement in offender reentry programs typically occurs through grant funding, which is available through a wide array of federal programs at the Departments of Justice, Labor, Education, and Health and Human Services. However, only a handful of grant programs in the federal government are designed explicitly for offender reentry purposes.

The Second Chance Act (P.L. 110-199) was enacted on April 9, 2008. The act expanded the existing offender reentry grant program at the Department of Justice and created a wide array of targeted grant-funded pilot programs.

Background

Over 95% of the prison population today will be released at some point in the future.[1] Since 2000, an average of 680,000 inmates have been released from state and federal prisons.[2] The Department of Justice's (DOJ's) Bureau of Justice Statistics (BJS) has estimated that two-thirds of all released prisoners will commit new offenses (recidivate) within three years of their release.[3] Many studies have indicated that reentry initiatives that combine work training and placement with counseling and housing assistance can reduce recidivism rates.[4]

According to the BJS, the average per prisoner cost of incarceration in state prison in 2001 was $62 per day, or $22,650 per year; costs for those incarcerated in federal prison were similar. Overall, the states spent $38 billion on their correctional systems in 2001, the most recent year for which data are available.[5]

Offender reentry includes all the activities and programming conducted to prepare ex-convicts to return safely to the community and to live as law-abiding citizens. Reentry programs are typically divided into three phases: programs that prepare offenders to reenter society while they are in prison, programs that connect ex-offenders with services immediately after they are released from prison, and programs that provide long-term support and supervision for ex-offenders as they settle into communities permanently. Offender reentry programs vary widely in range, scope, and methodology. The best-designed programs, according to the research in the field, are those that span all three phases.[6]

A Government Accountability Office (GAO) report also suggests that post-release planning should begin as early as possible, ideally as soon as an inmate is admitted into prison or even immediately after sentencing. Such planning could include helping the offender to develop the skills and knowledge base necessary to find a job and have access to education, such as General Equivalency Degree classes for those who have not completed high school, and either vocational training or college classes for those that have completed high school but have not entered into a career.[7]

As offenders approach their release date, the research suggests that reentry planning focus on connecting offenders with the community and workplace resources they will need to get established. Again, employment and access to education have been cited by many studies as two of the most important aspects contributing to the successful reintegration of ex-offenders into society.[8] Lastly, studies suggest it is important for the reentry process to continue as offenders' reintegrate into society. Indeed, for many offenders, the first few weeks of adjustment after release are actually less difficult than the longer period of community reintegration.9 In many cases, this period of time can span the entire three to five years that offenders are sometimes supervised in the community.[10]

Correctional System Statistics

To understand the issue of offender reentry, one must first understand the ways in which ex-offenders are released into the community. It is also worthwhile to analyze the population of individuals serving sentences in correctional facilities, because the number of offenders reentering the community is necessarily related to the number and type of offenders serving prison sentences. This section analyzes national data on the nation's correctional system.

Population in Correctional Facilities

The correctional system includes two main forms of detention: jails and prisons. Jails, also known as local lockups, are facilities generally used to temporarily detain individuals who have been arrested or charged with a crime but not usually convicted.[11] The jail population is thus extremely fluid, with individuals usually staying for a matter of weeks, and includes individuals who may never be convicted of a crime. Prisons, on the other hand, typically house individuals who have been convicted of a crime and sentenced to a term of one year or longer. For this reason, the prison population is less fluid than the jail population.[12]

The population serving time in correctional facilities has been steadily increasing since 1980, reaching its peak of approximately 2.3 million in 2008. The total correctional population in the U.S. actually decreased by approximately 16,000 inmates in 2009, though the overall reduction was the result of fewer jail inmates. Between 1980 and 2009, the number of people imprisoned in the United States increased, on average, 5.4% per year. However, since the beginning of the decade the number of people incarcerated has increased at a slower rate. The average annual increase in the number of people incarcerated in the United States was 2.0% between 2000 and 2009. Data from BJS show that the incarceration rate in the United States increased from 139 inmates per 100,000 people in 1980 to 502 inmates per 100,000 people in 2009.[13]

This indicates that the growth in the number of incarcerated inmates has exceeded the growth in the country's population. *Figure 1* shows the annual population in state and federal correctional facilities from 1980 to 2009 (the most recent data available).

Given the fact that 95% of all inmates will eventually return to the community,[14] the prison population has a direct impact on offender reentry. As the prison population grows, increasing numbers of ex-offenders are being released from correctional facilities.

Most of these ex-offenders are required to undergo some form of community supervision as part of their release. The following section explores the mechanisms and statistics surrounding the release of prisoners into the community.

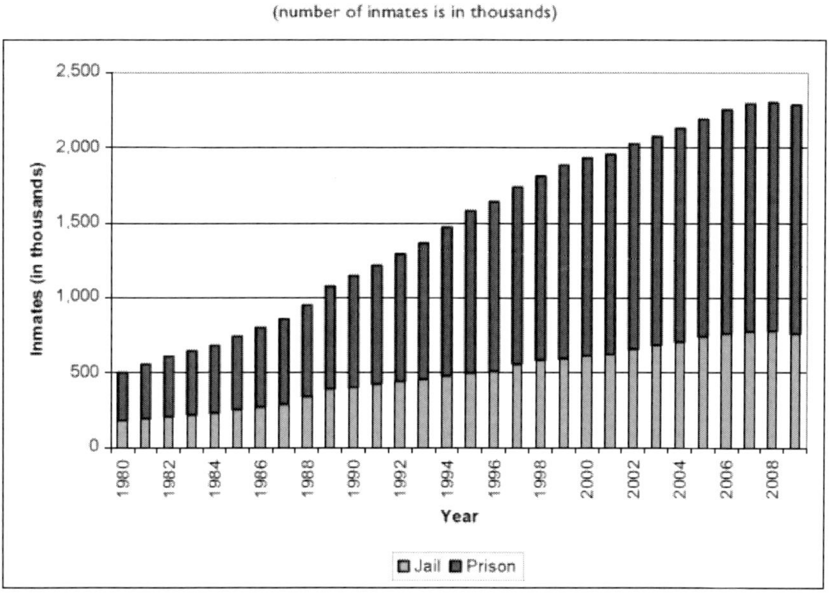

Source: CRS presentation of data from the Bureau of Justice Statistics.

Figure 1. Number of Inmates Incarcerated in the United States, 1980-2009.

Offenders under Community Supervision

Ex-offenders can be released into the community through a variety of different mechanisms. Some offenders never serve prison sentences and instead serve their sentence on probation in their communities under supervision. Others serve most of their sentences in correctional facilities but are then released on parole to finish their sentences in their communities under supervision. Lastly, some offenders serve out their entire sentences in correctional facilities and are released unconditionally into the community.

Probation

Individuals who are found guilty of committing a crime that is deemed not serious enough for imprisonment can be sentenced to serve their sentences under community supervision (probation). Offenders on probation typically must adhere to certain conditions and check in regularly with their probation officers. Violation of these conditions or failure to appear before their probation officers can lead to further criminal sanctions, including incarceration. In some instances, offenders can be sentenced to a mixed term of prison and probation.

Parole

Individuals who have served most of their sentences in a correctional facility are sometimes eligible to complete their sentences in the community under conditional supervision. While some states have a parole system in place, Congress abolished parole at the federal level effective in 1986. However, there is a small percentage of federal offenders who were sentenced prior to 1986 who are still eligible for parole. The conditions associated with parole can vary from case to case, but typically include drug testing and regular contact with a parole officer. Violations of these conditions can result in the parolee returning to prison to serve out the remaining portion of his or her sentence. There are two different kinds of parole: discretionary and mandatory.

Discretionary Parole

States that use parole boards to determine whether a prisoner should be released into the community have discretionary parole. Parole boards have the authority to conditionally release a prisoner into the community based on a statutory or an administrative determination that the prisoner is eligible.

Mandatory Parole

States that have statutory language determining when offenders should be released into the community have mandatory parole. Jurisdictions that use determinate sentencing[15] often include provisions specifying when inmates should be conditionally released from prison after serving a specified portion of their original sentences.

Figure 2 shows the number of offenders who were supervised in the community, either through probation or through parole, during the period from 1980 to 2009. It is important to note that between 1980 and 2009, parolees accounted for, on average, 16% of the overall population under community supervision. The growing state prison population has resulted in a concomitant growth in the overall population of offenders under community supervision. Interestingly, however, the growth rate of individuals under community supervision has been lagging behind the growth rate of individuals in correctional facilities. This is likely due to the fact that a growing number of offenders are being released directly into the community without any form of supervision. *Figure 2* shows that the number of offenders under community supervision increased by approximately 275% from 1980 to 2009; this contrasts with the overall prison population, shown in Figure 1, which grew by approximately 355% during this period.

(number of offenders is in millions)

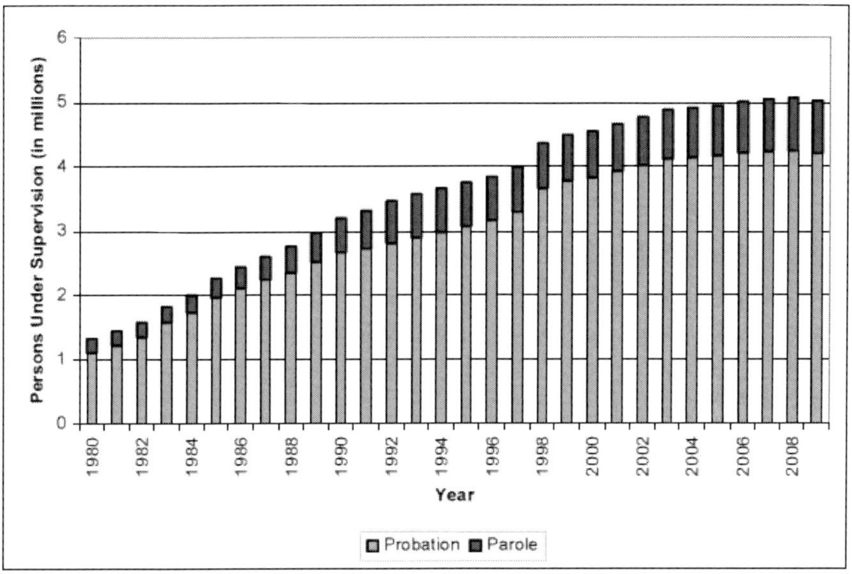

Source: CRS presentation of data from the Bureau of Justice Statistics.

Figure 2. Number of Offenders Under Community Supervision, 1980-2009.

The relationship between the prison and parole populations is an important one for a number of reasons. Offenders serving their sentences in prison have generally committed more serious crimes than offenders who serve their sentences in jail or on probation; as previously noted, the prison population typically includes individuals sentenced to more than a year of time. Parolees, meanwhile, often return to the community after a prolonged period of incarceration and usually face a period of adjustment.

Figure 3 shows the relationship between annual changes in the prison population and the parole population. *Figure 3* shows a differentiation between the period from 1981 to 1992, when the annual increase in the parole population generally outstripped the annual increase in the prison population, and the period from 1993 to 2005, when the obverse has largely been true. This is interesting for a number of reasons. The population of offenders on parole is, by definition, a subset of the population of offenders in prison: to get parole, one has to pass through the prison system. The fact that, in general, the population in prison has been increasing at a faster rate than the population on parole over the past 17 years suggests that fewer prisoners are being released before the end of their sentences; this corresponds with the sentencing reform efforts implemented by many states in the 1980s and early 1990s and the growing use of truth-insentencing laws by states. Truth-in-sentencing laws require that offenders serve a substantial portion of their sentences (usually three-quarters), thereby reducing discrepancies between the sentence imposed and the actual time served in prison.16 Additionally, the discrepancy between the annual growth of the parole and prison populations in the 1990s is also a result of the fact that prison sentences have become longer because of the enactment of mandatory minimum sentencing laws by most states. Taken together, these factors could suggest that the parole population may begin to grow faster than the prison population in coming years as the longer sentences that have been issued over the past two decades come closer to being completed.

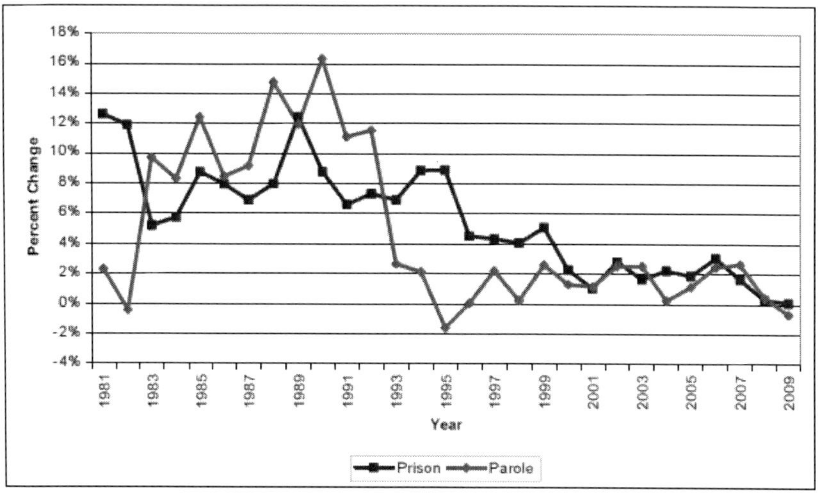

Source: CRS presentation of data from the Bureau of Justice Statistics.

Figure 3. Annual Change in the Prison and Parole Population.

Recidivism

Recidivism is often defined as the rearrest, reconviction, or reincarceration of an ex-offender within a given time frame. As a result of this broad definition of recidivism, most studies include technical violations of an offender's parole or probation (such as failing a drug test or not showing up for a meeting, for example) within their general recidivism statistics. Rearrest statistics also include individuals who are found innocent of the charges. For these reasons, some studies have focused on reincarceration with a new prison sentence as a more accurate recidivism statistic, arguing that technical violations are really an extension of an offender's original prison term and not a newly committed crime. Essentially, there are two competing philosophies about what recidivism should mean.[17] On the one hand are those who argue that any new contact with the criminal justice system, no matter how minor, should be considered recidivism on the part of an ex-offender.[18] On the other hand are those who argue that recidivism should be more narrowly defined as the commission of a new crime, resulting in a new sentence, by an ex-offender.[19] What one includes in the definition of recidivism has a substantial impact on the rate of recidivism reported.

Regardless of what definition is used, recidivism is a difficult subject to study. Tracking recidivism involves following the cases of individuals for a number of years and relying on state or national-level data sets that contain inherent inaccuracies. For example, if an offender is released in California but commits a new crime in Maine, the researchers must be able to match those two records together to make a definitive statement about recidivism. This match is typically done by consulting the FBI's master database of convictions; however, as we will see later, this database contains omissions that may affect the results of recidivism studies. A number of studies have been conducted on this issue, and most states have calculated their own recidivism rates. However, there is a dearth of current national-level statistics on recidivism by ex-offenders. The two main national-level studies that have been conducted over the last 15 years are outlined below.

Bureau of Justice Statistics 1994 Recidivism Study

One of the most comprehensive national-level recidivism study to date was conducted by the Bureau of Justice Statistics (BJS) and dates back to 1994.[20] The BJS study examined the rearrest, reconviction, and reincarceration of prisoners from 15 states three years after their release in 1994.[21] The study tracked 272,111 prisoners, or almost two-thirds of all the prisoners released from state prisons in 1994.

Figure 4 below summarizes the main findings of the BJS recidivism study. After three years, the study found that over two-thirds (67.5%) of the prisoners released had been rearrested for a new offense. Almost half (46.9%)

of the prisoners had been reconvicted of a new crime. Just over half (51.8%) of the prisoners released were back in prison either because they had been resentenced to prison for a new crime they had committed (25.4%) or because they had violated some technical provision of their release (26.4%).[22] The BJS study therefore showed that more than half of ex-offenders who return to prison do so because of technical violations of their parole or probation rather than the commission of a new crime. It is important to note that the BJS study did not include information on what percentage of ex-offenders were serving time in local jails; however, as previously noted, local jails feature a fluid population of inmates who usually reside there for a brief period of time and may not be convicted of the crime for which they are being held.

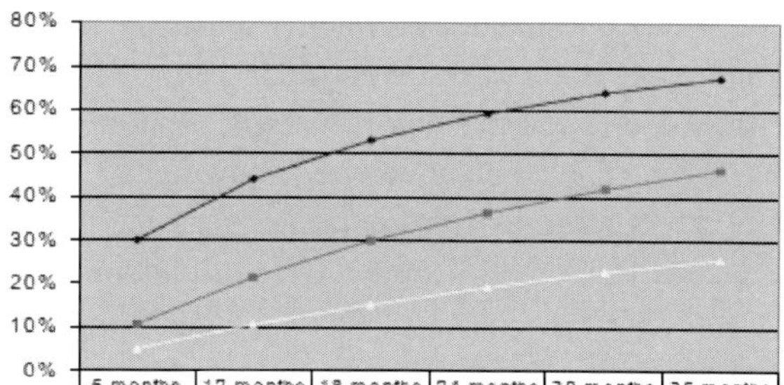

	6 months	12 months	18 months	24 months	30 months	36 months
Rearrested	30%	44%	53%	59%	64%	67%
Reconvicted	11%	22%	30%	36%	42%	46%
Returned to prison with a new prison sentence	5%	11%	15%	19%	23%	25%

Source: CRS analysis of Bureau of Justice Statistics data.

Notes: Because of missing data, prisoners released in Ohio were excluded from the calculation of "Percent reconvicted." The category "New prison sentence" includes sentences to state and federal penitentiaries but does not include sentences to local jails. Because of missing data, prisoners released in Ohio and Virginia were excluded from the calculation of "Percent returned to prison with a new prison sentence."

Figure 4. Bureau of Justice Statistics Recidivism Study.

Pew Recidivism Study

The Pew Center on the States (Pew), in collaboration with the Association of State Correctional Administrators (ASCA), surveyed each state's department of corrections in an attempt to collect a single source of state-by-state recidivism data.[23] The survey asked states to provide 36-month recidivism rates for offenders released in 1999 and 2004.[24] Thirty-three states provided data for the 1999 release cohort and 41 states provided data for the 2004 release cohort. Pew reported that the data allowed them to analyze recidivism trends in 33 states.

Pew found that, when only considering the states that reported data on both cohorts, the recidivism rate for inmates released in 1999 was 45.4%, and for inmates released in 2004 it was 43.3%. The recidivism rate decreased slightly between 1999 and 2004 even though nearly 64,000 more inmates were released in 2004 than in 1999. Of the offenders in the 1999 cohort, 19.9% of them were reincarcerated for a new crime, while 25.5% were returned to prison for a technical violation of post-incarceration supervision. Of the offenders in the 2004 cohort, 22.3% of them were reincarcerated for a new crime, while 21% were returned to prison for a technical violation of post-incarceration supervision. Pew also compared reported recidivism rates for inmates released in 1999 and 2004 from the 15 states included in the 1994 BJS recidivism study (see above) and found that recidivism rates have remained relatively stable over time. The 1999 and 2004 recidivism rates for the states included in the 1994 BJS study (excluding California) were 39.7% and 38.5%, respectively, which is similar to the 40.1% recidivism rate calculated by BJS (if California is excluded).[25]

United States Sentencing Commission Study

The United States Sentencing Commission (USSC) studied the recidivism rates of a random sample of 6,062 offenders who were sentenced under federal sentencing guidelines in FY1992. The recidivism information was derived from the "RAP" sheet criminal history repository maintained by the FBI's Criminal Justice Information Services Division, which has certain limitations (discussed below). The USSC study examined the relationship between the offenders' sentences and recidivism rates. The USSC developed the Criminal History Category (CHC) based on a review of prediction measures that were popularized in a National Academy of Sciences study in the 1980s.[26] Generally, an offender's prior criminal record will determine which CHC they are placed in. There are six CHC levels; an offender's placement within these levels is determined by a points system based on their prior contacts with the criminal justice system. Points are awarded for prior convictions, for violations of technical provisions of their judicial supervision (e.g., bail or parole), and for violent crimes. Juvenile and special court martial convictions are also counted. The higher the CHC, the more severe the offender's criminal history is.[27]

Figure 5 summarizes the USSC's findings. Generally, the study showed that an offender's criminal history was strongly associated with the likelihood of the offender recidivating after being released. The more prior convictions or the more serious the nature of the offender's crimes, the more likely the offender was to recidivate. The study also showed that the definition of recidivism had a large impact on the resulting statistics. For example, for the most hardened ex-offenders, general recidivism, which includes *any* contact with the criminal justice system, was at 55% after two years. Over this same period, the re-conviction rate for the most hardened ex-offenders was only 15%. This discrepancy shows that the definition of recidivism is important; even for the most hardened ex-offenders, the reconviction rate was relatively low compared with the general recidivism.

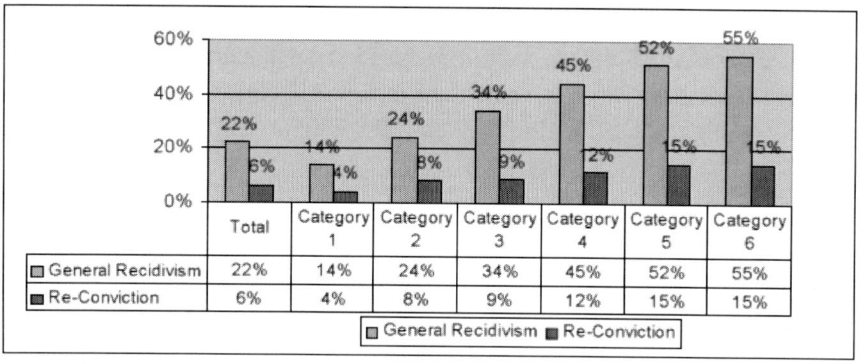

	Total	Category 1	Category 2	Category 3	Category 4	Category 5	Category 6
General Recidivism	22%	14%	24%	34%	45%	52%	55%
Re-Conviction	6%	4%	8%	9%	12%	15%	15%

Source: CRS presentation of United States Sentencing Commission data.

Figure 5. United States Sentencing Commission Recidivism Findings.

National Recidivism Study Limitations

The data used in the BJS, Pew and USSC studies come from official records maintained by the states' and the Federal Bureau of Investigation's (FBI's) official criminal history repositories. These repositories understate the actual recidivism levels to some unknown extent because they rely on local police agencies and courts to supply them with notifying documents. These documents are not always filed by local police departments or courts, however. In addition, if the offender provided a different name or a fraudulent identity document to police, and this misinformation was not discovered, they would likely not be captured by the data. Lastly, even if the criminal is correctly identified and the document is sent to the repository, the repository may not be able to match the person identified in the document with their records. This could occur, for example, if the document that has been submitted is filled out incorrectly or is illegible.

Moreover, as previously noted, there is some debate about what kind of outcome measure should be included when measuring recidivism. Should recidivism statistics include any contact with the criminal justice system by an ex-offender? Or should recidivism statistics be limited to the commission of crimes by ex-offenders that result in new convictions or new sentences? Both the BJS and the USSC studies showed wide differentials between general recidivism, which includes any contact with the criminal justice system, and re-conviction rates for new crimes. The length of the follow-up period will also play a role in the recidivism statistics that are generated. Because of the costs and difficulties associated with studying recidivism, most studies follow ex-offenders for two or three years. There is a dearth of information concerning what happens to ex-offenders beyond the three-year window that is typically studied. For all of these reasons, caution should be taken when attempting to draw conclusions about the efficacy of policy measures based solely on recidivism statistics. When using recidivism statistics to evaluate a program, it is important to understand exactly what is included in the definition of recidivism. For example, consider the following hypothetical scenario: a program is evaluated and shows significant decreases in the number of ex-offenders that are convicted of new crimes and sentenced to new prison terms; however, the number of ex-offenders arrested for violating their parole actually increased. Was this program successful or not? Did it make society safer or not? This may well be an unlikely scenario, but it calls attention to the fact that recidivism may mean different things to different people. While recidivism statistics remain the best information available concerning whether ex-offenders come into contact with the criminal justice system after being released from prison and what the nature of that contact is, they are but one factor to be considered when evaluating the efficacy of a program, because of the concerns outlined above.

Importance of Considering Other Outcome Measures

While recidivism has traditionally been the most widely used metric used to determine the effectiveness of correctional and reentry programs, it is important to note here that other outcome measures can help determine whether an offender's reintegration into society is succeeding. Measures of attachment to social institutions, such as employment, involvement in community activities, church-going, and participation in support groups, can be important bellwethers of an offender's transition to the community.28 For example, one study of drug court29 participants showed that drug courts reduce drug use among their participants and that children born to drug court participants are less likely to be born addicted to drugs.30 Given the high societal costs associated with substance-dependent infants, for that particular program, recidivism was arguably not the most important outcome measure that could have been considered. To give policy makers a better idea of what happens to ex-offenders, program evaluations are best focused on the entire universe of activities in which ex-offenders engage. A potential issue for Congress could be whether these alternate measures of an offender reentry program's effectiveness in fostering reintegration within the community should be considered when deciding how best to allocate grant funding and other government resources. A related issue could be whether reporting on these alternate outcome measures should be required of programs receiving federal grant funding.

Lack of Current Federal Recidivism Statistics

As previously noted, the only national-level recidivism statistics concerning the reentry of prisoners into the community are more than a decade old. These studies showed that over two-thirds of ex-offenders had come into contact with the legal system—either through a new arrest, a violation of the terms of their release, or a new conviction—within three years of their release. However, there are no current national-level recidivism statistics. While a number of states have conducted studies of their prisoners' recidivism, the lack of national-level statistics poses a challenge for policy makers as they consider the issue of offender reentry. Without a current, national-level analysis of which ex-offenders are more likely to recidivate, it is difficult to target funding to offender reentry programs that address the at-risk population. Indeed, much of the offender reentry literature being published today continues to cite the Bureau of Justice Statistics study from the mid-1990s when referring to recidivism. A potential issue of interest for Congress may be whether a new, national-level recidivism study is needed to better understand the current trends in recidivism and to better target federal funding to the ex-offenders that are most likely to re-offend.

OFFENDER REENTRY: A BRIEF LITERATURE REVIEW

Virtually all prisoners currently being detained in secure facilities will, someday, be released into the community, and more offenders are transitioning into the community today than ever before. Offender reentry is a complex issue that touches on a wide range of social and governmental networks and programs. Offender reentry policies can vary significantly from state to state, and from community to community within particular states. The policies affecting prisoners and the kinds of programs available to them both in and out of prison depend on a variety of factors, including the availability of funding for social programs within states and communities and the number of private non-profit and religious organizations operating in a given community. The federal government plays a supporting role through the numerous grant funding opportunities (discussed below). Complicating factors affecting how offender reentry works in a given community can include

- the varying types of sentences handed down,
- the different kinds of release mechanisms available to judges,
- the types of programs provided in prisons by correctional systems,
- the intensity of supervision provided or required by the parole or releasing agency,
- the family and community support available to the offender,
- the kinds of social services available in the offender's community, and
- the status of the local economy and the offender's ability to obtain employment.[31]

Offender Reentry Defined

Before we can discuss offender reentry programs, however, it is useful to comment on what constitutes offender reentry. Some observers note that offender reentry is the natural byproduct of incarceration, because all prisoners who are not sentenced to life in prison and who do not die in prison will reenter the community at some point. According to this school of thought, reentry is not a program or some kind of legal status but rather a process that almost all offenders will undergo.[32] A variant on this approach to reentry is the concept that offender reentry, "simply defined, includes all activities and programming conducted to prepare ex-convicts to return safely to the community and to live as law abiding citizens."[33] The basic idea here is that every activity and process that a prisoner undergoes while in the judicial and correctional systems will have some nexus with their reentry into the community.

Although this broad definition of reentry certainly encompasses all the activities that may impinge on or affect a prisoner's reentry into society, it may be a cumbersome one for the purposes of crafting and evaluating government policies. For example, it is difficult, if not impossible, to measure the outcome of a reentry program if one includes in the definition of reentry every activity that a prisoner undergoes during his time in the criminal justice system. This has led many in the field to focus on a more narrow and thus more manageable definition of reentry. This more narrow definition is often stated in two parts: correctional programs that focus on the transition to the community (such as prerelease, work release, halfway houses, or other programs specifically aiming at reentry) and programs that have initiated some form of treatment (such as substance abuse, life skills, education, or mental health) in prison that is linked to community programs that will continue the treatment once the prisoner has been released.[34] Narrowing the definition of reentry thusly allows policy makers to focus on programs that expressly aim to manage the transition from detention to the community.

Program Effectiveness: The "What Works" Literature

Compared with other social science fields, there has been a relative lack of rigorously designed studies on the issue of offender reentry. Nevertheless, in recent years, there has been increasing attention on this issue and a number of new studies have been published. This has allowed academics to undertake some of the first broad meta-analyses[35] of offender reentry studies. Some of these studies have hewn closely to the "what works" paradigm created by University of Maryland researchers for a National Institute of Justice report to Congress.[36] This concept was adapted to the field of offender reentry in a 2003 St. Louis University Study.[37] The "what works" literature attempts to identify programs that are effective by creating a scoring system to evaluate studies based on whether they can be proven to have an impact. Inherent to this approach is the need to identify program evaluations that provide evidence concerning the effect the program had on certain outcome measures. The "what works" paradigm essentially focuses on whether studies have accomplished the following things:

- controlled for variables in their analysis that may have been the underlying cause of any observed connection between the program being studied and the outcome measures being analyzed;

- determined whether there are measurement errors resulting from problems with the study, including such things as participants being lost over time or low response rates to interview requests; and
- calculated the statistical power of the analysis to detect the program's effects on outcome measures. Included in this category are things such as sample size and the base rate of crime in the community.[38]

The "what works" model uses these core criteria to place studies into five distinct categories, with category 5 being the most scientifically rigorous, and thus considered most effective, studies.

The model then uses this criteria to identify programs that, based on the evidence considered, have been proven to work, programs that are promising, and programs that do not work.

Following is a brief discussion of the types of offender reentry programs that have been judged to be effective in the "what works" literature, as well as in other studies. It is important to note here that, just because a program has been reported to work in one location, or for a certain population, does not necessarily mean that it can be just as effective in other locations or among other populations.

A number of factors can impinge on a program's effectiveness in any given location. For example, while knowing that a program has worked in the past can provide a model or blueprint to guide policy practitioners in other locations, how a program is implemented is just as important to its ultimate success as the underlying model that it is based on.

The most effective model program can be compromised if it is not implemented properly. In addition, geographic, demographic, and other differences between locations can affect whether a program that succeeded in one place succeeds in another. Nevertheless, knowing that a program has worked in the past is of use to policy makers as they consider where to allocate funding and other resources.

Employment

There are a number of studies that demonstrate that employment is a fundamental component of the reentry process, and that ex-offenders who are able to find stable employment are much more likely to succeed in their rehabilitation than those who cannot find work.[39]

Several vocational and work programs were found to effectively reduce recidivism and improve the job-readiness of ex-offenders by the "what works" review.[40]

Drug Treatment

Drug rehabilitation and treatment have also been found to be effective by a number of different studies, including the "what works" literature. These studies showed that, for recidivism and drug-use relapse, drug treatment can significantly improve outcome measures. In general, programs that provide intensive treatment in prison, combined and integrated with aftercare programs, have been shown to be effective in reducing recidivism and substance abuse among their participants—especially for offenders with serious crime and substance abuse histories.[41]

Halfway House Programs

A number of programs that provide transitional housing for ex-offenders as they begin their transition into the community have been found to be effective. Offenders participating in halfway house programs were found to commit fewer and less severe offenses than those who did not participate. Participants also performed better on a range of other outcome measures, such as finding and holding a job, being self-supporting, and participating in self-improvement programs; however, these results were not statistically significant.[42]

Other Kinds of Programs

The "what works" review concluded that other programs were either not effective or had not been studied enough for firm conclusions to be drawn. Education programs, for example, were found to raise educational achievement scores but not to reduce recidivism. Pre-release programs and programs focusing on violent offenders and sex offenders showed some evidence that they were effective in reducing recidivism, but few of these kinds of studies made it through the selection process. This precluded any firm conclusions from being drawn about these kinds of programs and pointed to the need for more evaluations.[43]

Limitations of the "What Works" Literature

One of the main limitations associated with the "what works" literature is the dearth of studies that meet its rigorous requirements. For example, the offender reentry study cited above was only able to identify 32 studies that met its selection criteria. Only 19 of these program evaluations contained a comparison, or control, group, and of these, only two were randomized control trials.[44] This has led some to question whether the programs identified to work by this literature review are, in fact, effective.[45] Moreover, most of the studies identified by the "what works" literature evaluate program effectiveness based almost entirely on recidivism. As previously noted, some believe other outcome measures may be just as important in deciding whether a program has been effective in reintegrating ex-offenders into their communities. Lastly, evaluations that incorporate random assignment and provide statistically rigorous results are, by and large, expensive. This means that policy makers are often confronted with hard decisions concerning whether to fund additional services or evaluations of existing programs.

Conclusion

After reviewing the available literature, some patterns appear to emerge. Many of the programs that have been proven to be effective share some of the same attributes, regardless of whether they focus on vocational training, substance abuse prevention, mental health services, or alternative housing. The attributes shared by most of these programs include the following:

- they start during institutional placement, but take place mostly in the community;
- they are intensive in nature, lasting typically at least six months;
- they focus services on individuals determined to be at high risk of recidivating through the use of risk-assessment classifications; and
- if they are treatment programs, they use cognitive-behavioral treatment techniques, matching particular therapists and programs to the specific learning characteristics of the offenders.[46]

Federal Offender Reentry Programs

A wide array of federal programs and grants can be used by states to support offender reentry. Many of these programs participated in the federal government-wide Serious and Violent Offender Reentry Initiative (SVORI), a four-year, $300 million initiative that pooled the federal offender reentry resources of the Departments of Justice, Labor, Education, and Housing and Urban Development in order to reduce recidivism.[47] This program officially concluded in FY2005. More recently, the Office of Justice Programs (OJP) announced it had formed a partnership with the Department of Labor known as the Prisoner Reentry Initiative (PRI). The PRI program, like SVORI, is an interagency effort to coordinate the provision of federal funding for the reintegration of offenders into the community. While funding opportunities for offender reentry programs exist within the purpose areas of many broad grant programs, only one grant program (PRI) is specifically tailored for offender reentry within the federal government. Both the SVORI and the PRI utilized the authorization outlined above; however, as previously noted, the authorization expired in FY2005 but the program continued to receive appropriations in FY2006 and FY2007. Following is a brief description of the main federal programs that have been used to help state and local entities to fund activities relating to the reintegration of ex-offenders into local communities. It is important to note that some of these programs may no longer be receiving funding; these programs are identified below. Other programs that are currently funded may not provide funding for offender reentry purposes every fiscal year. Nevertheless, these programs have been included to provide a comprehensive look at the universe of federal resources that could be used for offender reentry purposes.

Offender Reentry Programs at the Department of Justice (DOJ)

The Office of Justice Programs within DOJ oversees a wide array of grant programs that include support for offender reentry programs or activities among the purpose areas eligible for funding. Some of these programs may be more focused on offender reentry than others, but all of them can be used for offender reentry purposes.

The Serious and Violent Offender Reentry Initiative

The Office of Justice Programs (OJP) coordinated a federal offender reentry pilot program for adult offenders, the Serious and Violent Offender Reentry Initiative (SVORI). This program focused on coordinating the way federal agencies distribute existing offender reentry funding. The main federal agencies involved were the Departments of Justice, Labor, Education, and Housing and Urban Development. As part of SVORI, their objective was to help state and local agencies navigate the wide array of existing state formula and block grants and to assist the states and communities to leverage those resources to create comprehensive offender reentry programs. The program distributed $110 million to 69 grantees and concluded in FY2005.

A evaluation of SVORI programs was released in December 2009.[48] The evaluation, among other things, evaluated the post-release outcomes of participants in 16 programs (12 adult and 4 juvenile) in 14 states.[49] The evaluation found that there was little difference in the reported reentry programming needs between offenders who participated in SVORI programs and those who did not participate. Inmates who participated in SVORI programs were more likely to receive reentry programming and services than those who did not participate, but not all SVORI program participants received programming or services. The researchers also found that the provision of services for program participants was below the expressed need for services. Moreover, the provision of services decreased after the inmates were released from confinement. The researchers found that adults who participated in the SVORI program were moderately less likely than non-participants to find housing and employment, not use drugs, and self-report less criminal behavior, but the improvements on these measures did not translate into lower levels of reincarceration. Juvenile males who participated in SVORI programs were more likely than nonparticipants to have a job with benefits 15 months after being released, but there was no significant difference between program participants and non-participants in terms of substance abuse, physical health, mental health, or recidivism.

The Prisoner Reentry Initiative

The Prisoner Reentry Initiative (PRI) appears to have been instituted as a replacement for the SVORI program. According to OJP, the PRI provides funding for model offender reentry programs that focus on providing services and assistance during the three phases of offender reentry: at detention facilities, just prior to and after the offender's release, and during an ex-offender's long-term transition to the community. Congress discontinued funding the PRI after FY2008.

Second Chance Act of 2007

The Second Chance Act of 2007 (P.L. 110-199)[50] expands the current offender reentry grant program at DOJ, replacing the four purpose areas currently eligible for funding with new purpose areas spanning every phase of the offender reentry process. Applicants for these grants are subject to a number of requirements, including submitting a reentry strategic plan with their application, describing the long-term strategy, and providing a detailed implementation schedule, among other things. The act requires that states and localities match 50% of the federal funds provided; up to half of this state match (or 25% of the overall total funding) can be composed of in-kind contributions. The act also creates some new demonstration grant programs, including

- grants for state and local reentry courts;
- grants for drug treatment diversion programs;
- grants to expand substance-abuse programs for prisoners and ex-offenders; and
- grants to expand the use of career training programs and mentoring programs.

Since FY2009, funding for reentry programs has been appropriated pursuant to the grant programs authorized by the Second Chance Act.

Table 1. Direct Appropriations for DOJ Reentry Grant Programs

Fiscal Year	Appropriation
2001	$30,000,000
2002	14,934,000
2003	14,934,000
2004	5,000,000
2005	10,000,000
2006	8,000,000[a]
2007	14,879,140
2008	11,750,000
2009	25,000,000[b]
2010	100,000,000[c]
2011	82,834,000[d]
2012	63,000,000[e]

Source: FY2001 appropriation taken from H.Rept. 106-1005; FY2002 appropriation taken from H.Rept. 107- 278; FY2003 appropriation taken from H.Rept. 108-10; FY2004 appropriation taken from H.Rept. 108-401; FY2005 appropriation taken from H.Rept. 108-792; FY2006 appropriation taken from H.Rept. 109-272; FY2007 appropriation was provided by the Community Oriented Policing Services Office; FY2008 appropriation was taken from P.L. 110-161; FY2009 appropriation was taken from P.L. 111-8; FY2010 appropriation taken from H.Rept. 111-366; FY2011 appropriation based on a CRS analysis of the text of P.L. 112-10: FY2012 appropriation taken from H.Rept. 112-284.

Note: As previously noted, DOJ replaced the SVORI program with the PRI program in FY2006; however as both of these grant programs were implemented under the authority granted by the reentry program codified at 42 U.S.C. 3797w, they have been combined in this table. It is important to note as well that reentry funding has been appropriated in other federal agencies' budgets.

[a] In FY2006, there was also $5 million appropriated for reentry grant programs under the Community Oriented Policing Services account and $3 million appropriated for faith-based reentry programs under the Federal Prison System. These totals have been combined in this table, but it should be noted that they are for different programs.

[b] This amount includes $15 million for adult and juvenile offender re-entry demonstration programs which were reauthorized by section 101 of the Second Chance Act (P.L. 110-199). This amount also includes $10 million for grants for non-profit organizations to provide mentoring and transitional services to ex-offenders. This grant program was authorized by section 211 of the Second Chance Act.

[c] This amount includes $37 million for adult and juvenile offender re-entry demonstration programs which were reauthorized by section 101 of the Second Chance Act. This amount also includes $10 million for state, tribal, and local re-entry courts (authorized by section 111 of the Second Chance Act); $7.5 million for family-based substance abuse treatment programs (authorized by section 113 of the Second Chance Act); $2.5 million to evaluate and improve education at prisons, jails, and juvenile facilities (authorized by section 114 of the Second Chance Act); $5 million for technology careers training demonstration grants (authorized by section 115 of the Second Chance Act); $13 million for offender re-entry substance abuse and criminal justice collaboration (authorized by section 201 of the Second Chance Act); $15 million for grants for mentoring and transitional services (authorized by section 211 of the Second Chance Act); and $10 million for prisoner re-entry research (authorized by section 245 of the Second Chance Act).

[d] This amount includes $30.6 million for adult and juvenile offender re-entry demonstration programs that were reauthorized by section 101 of the Second Chance Act. This amount also includes $8.3 million for state, tribal, and local re-entry courts (authorized by section 111 of the Second Chance Act); $6.2 million for family-based substance abuse treatment programs (authorized by section 113 of the Second Chance Act); $2.1 million to evaluate and improve education at prisons, jails, and juvenile facilities (authorized by section 114 of the Second Chance Act); $4.1 million for technology careers training demonstration grants (authorized by section 115 of the Second Chance Act); $10.8 million for offender re-entry substance abuse and criminal justice collaboration (authorized by section 201 of the Second Chance Act); $12.4 million for grants for mentoring and transitional services (authorized by section 211 of the Second Chance Act); and $8.3 million for prisoner re-entry research (authorized by section 245 of the Second Chance Act).

[e] For FY2012, Congress did not specify how funding for the Second Chance Act had to be divided amongst the programs authorized by the act. Rather, Congress left the decision on how to allocate funding amongst the programs authorized by the act to the Office of Justice Programs.

Offender Reentry Programs at Other Federal Agencies

As previously mentioned, many federal departments provide funding through a wide array of programs and block grants, which can be used by states for offender reentry. The following list is not meant to be an exhaustive one, but it does capture many programs run by other departments that can be used to support state offender reentry initiatives.

The Department of Labor (DOL)

The Workforce Investment Act[51] (WIA) of 1998 (P.L. 105-220) authorized a nationwide system of workforce development programs, America's Workforce Network, that provides information and services to connect youths and adults with employers.[52] These programs, which can be used by ex-offenders, provide services such as skills-training and job-placement. DOL also instituted a Young Offender Reentry Demonstration Grant Program, which provides funds to communities for offender reentry programs for offenders aged 14 to 21 who are already in the criminal justice system or are considered high-risk. This program focuses on job-training, education, substance-abuse treatment, mental health care, housing assistance, and family support services.

In addition, DOL maintains two programs that provide incentives for companies to hire ex-offenders. The Work Opportunity Tax Credits program[53] provides up to $2,400 in tax credits to companies for every former offender they hire,[54] and the Federal Bonding Program[55] allows companies who cannot obtain bonding or insurance from their own providers to bond ex-offenders for up to $25,000 for up to six months.[56]

The Department of Education (DOE)

Numerous DOE programs can be used by states to help fund or provide technical support for offender reentry programs that focus on education. The Office of Vocational and Adult Education provides several different programs for offender reentry. The Lifeskills for State and Local Inmates Program provides funding for demonstration projects to reduce recidivism through educational services before inmates are discharged into the community.[57] The Grants to States for Workplace and Community Transition Training for Incarcerated Youth Offenders funds postsecondary education and vocational training to people under the age of 25 from five years before their release to one year post-release.[58] Title II of the Workforce Investment Act, Adult Education and Family Literacy, also authorized funding to be appropriated for basic skills instruction; up to 10% of the funds can be used for institutionalized offenders or for ex-offenders in community programs. In addition, the Perkins State Grant Program allows states to use up to 1% of their funds to serve offenders in institutions.[59]

The Department of Housing and Urban Development (HUD)

HUD funds a variety of programs that help states and local governments to support housing programs. The Community Development Block Grant Program aims to assist states in developing viable urban communities. Funds are allocated by formula to the states, and communities and grantees have significant discretion concerning how to allocate their federal funding—including using some funds to provide housing for ex-offenders.[60]

The Department of Health and Human Services (DHHS)

DHHS provides funding for a multitude of programs that can be used to help offender reentry programs through the Substance Abuse and Mental Health Services Agency[61] (SAMHSA) and the Office of Community Services. These programs include the Recovery Community Support Program, which targets people and families recovering from drug abuse and addiction, and several block grant programs. SAMHSA also funds a program that specifically targets offender reentry known as the Young Offender Reentry Program (YORP). The YORP provides funding for state, tribal, and local governments, as well as community based non-profit organizations, to expand substance abuse treatment and supervision programs for juvenile and young adult offenders re-entering the community.62 Funds for DHHS programs may be used to provide substance abuse or mental health services for offenders on parole or probation. However, DHHS funds may not used to provide services to incarcerated offenders.[63]

Coordination between Federal Agencies

There are a number of entities that bring together offender reentry professionals from state and local governments, non-profit organizations, and academic institutions, including the Reentry Policy Council founded by the Council of State Governments and the Reentry Roundtable hosted by the Urban Institute. Both of these organizations attempt to bolster information sharing about best practices and funding opportunities and coordination between the various state and local agencies and stake-holders within the offender reentry field. However, the extent to which the various federal agencies with grant programs that can be used for offender reentry purposes coordinate their efforts is currently unclear.

While the Serious and Violent Offender Reentry Initiative, as previously noted, reportedly brought together stakeholders from the Departments of Justice, Labor, Education, and Health and Human Services, that pilot program ended in FY2005. Despite the collaboration noted above, it is unclear to what extent these various departments have been coordinating the reentry funding available through their various other grant programs. This raises a potential issue concerning the extent to which duplication of resources is currently occurring across the federal government. A number of the grant programs identified above share purpose areas or can be used to fund similar activities. This could create a certain measure of confusion among state and local entities applying for offender reentry grant funding. There is currently no federal entity legislatively charged with coordinating federal offender reentry programs and services across the federal government. A potential issue for Congress could include whether some form of coordinating council or federal offender reentry clearinghouse should be created to provide supervision and oversight to the federal government's offender reentry efforts.

CONCLUSION

Over the past two and a half decades, the prison population and the number of ex-offenders being released into the community have been increasing. The increasing number of ex-offenders entering the community has put pressure on public policy makers to provide treatments and services that will smooth the reintegration process while reducing recidivism. When deciding what programs to fund, policy makers often focus on reducing recidivism. The focus on reducing recidivism, however, is complicated by the fact that there are different definitions of recidivism. For example, the last major national-level study showed that two-thirds of ex-offenders came into contact with the legal system and that about half were back in prison within three years of their release. However, only a quarter of the ex-offenders ended up in prison for having committed new crimes; another quarter were back in prison for technical violations of their release (such as failing a drug test). Whether technical violations should be considered a measure of recidivism or whether recidivism should be confined to the commission of new crimes has engendered much debate within the criminal justice field.

While the emphasis on reducing recidivism is important, programs should also be evaluated based on other outcome measures such as their ability to connect ex-offenders with jobs, services, and institutions in their communities. The best available research has shown that there are a number of services that can help ex-offenders reconnect with their communities and lower recidivism, including programs focusing on providing vocational training, substance abuse prevention, mental health services, and alternative housing. The most successful programs focus on high-risk offenders, are intensive in nature, begin during institutional placement, and take place mostly in the community. However, a relative lack of scientifically rigorous research has made it difficult to draw definitive conclusions about which programs are most effective.

As Congress considers this issue, a number of policy issues may be assessed, including whether the current federal grant programs are adequate or whether new programs should be created, whether there is a need for more current national-level recidivism data, whether enough coordination of the many programs that may be used to help ex-offenders is occurring within the federal government, whether more evaluations of offender reentry programs are needed, and whether funding will be appropriated for the programs and activities that were authorized by the Second Chance Act.

APPENDIX. SECTION-BY-SECTION COMPARISON OF THE SECOND CHANCE ACT

The Second Chance Act, P.L. 110-199, was passed by the House on November 13, 2007, and by the Senate on March 11, 2008. The act was signed into law on April 9, 2008. Following is a section-by-section analysis of the act's provisions.

Amendments to Current Offender Reentry Grant Program (§101)

The Second Chance Act reauthorized and expanded the adult and juvenile offender state and local offender reentry demonstration projects codified at 42 U.S.C. 3797w(b-c). The act replaced the four current purpose areas eligible for funding with seven broad purpose areas:

- educational, literacy, vocational, and job placement services;
- substance abuse treatment and services, including programs that start in placement and continue through the community;
- programs that provide comprehensive supervision and offer services in the community, including programs that provide housing assistance and mental and physical health services;
- programs that focus on family integration during and after placement for both offenders and their families;
- mentoring programs that start in placement and continue into the community;
- programs that provide victim-appropriate services, including those that promote the timely payment of restitution by offenders and those that offer services (such as security or counseling) to victims when offenders are released; and
- programs that protect communities from dangerous offenders, including developing and implementing the use of risk assessment tools to determine when offenders should be released from prison.

Applicants for these grants are subjected to a number of requirements, including submitting a reentry strategic plan with their application, describing the long-term strategy, providing a detailed implementation schedule, identifying the local government's role in the plan, and describing the "evidence based methodology and outcome measures" that are used to evaluate the programs and "provide valid measures" of the program's impact.

The act allows the Attorney General (AG) to make grants for these programs if the applications received meet the following conditions:

- they are explicitly supported by the chief executive of the unit of government applying for the funding;
- they extensively discuss the role that the various law enforcement entities involved in the reentry process will have in the program;
- they provide extensive evidence of collaboration among the state and local health, housing, child welfare, education, substance abuse, victims services, employment, and law enforcement agencies;
- they provide a plan for analyzing any statutory, regulatory, or other hurdles that may exist to reintegrating offenders into the community; and

- they include a reentry taskforce as described below to carry out the activities funded under the grant.

The act requires applicants to develop a comprehensive strategic reentry plan that contains measurable five-year performance outcomes, with the goal of reducing recidivism by 50% over this period. As a condition of funding, applicants are also required to create offender reentry taskforces that would integrate the prime offender reentry stake-holders in their communities in order to pool resources, facilitate data-collection, and reduce recidivism. Grantees are also required to submit annual reports to DOJ that identify the specific progress made toward achieving their strategic performance outcomes, and may be eligible for future grants if they demonstrate adequate progress towards reducing recidivism by 10% over a two-year period.

In awarding grants under this program, the AG is directed to prioritize applications that

- focus on geographic areas with a disproportionate population of ex-offenders;
- include input from non-profit organizations, consultation with victims and ex-offenders, and coordinate with families;
- demonstrate effective case management in order to provide comprehensive and continuous services during reentry;
- review the adjudications process for parole violations in the applicant's criminal justice system;
- provide for an independent evaluation of the program, including, to the extent practicable, the use of random assignment; and
- target high risk offenders through the use of validated assessment tools.

Additionally, the act establishes a National Adult and Juvenile Offender Reentry Resource Center by authorizing the AG to make a grant available to an eligible organization.

The selected organization are directed to provide education, training, and technical assistance to states and other governments in order to collect and disseminate data and best practices in offender reentry, including the use of evaluation tools and other measures to assess and document performance. Up to 4% of the authorized level of funding can be used to establish and run this center.

The act authorizes $55 million in both FY2009 and FY2010 for these programs and limits funding for technical assistance and training to between 2% and 3% of the overall total appropriated.

The total federal share of funding for these grants is limited to 50%; however, up to 50% of the state and local matching funds (i.e., 25% of the overall grant) could be fulfilled through in-kind contributions of goods or services.

Improvement of the Residential Substance Abuse Treatment for State Offenders Program (§102)

This provision requires states receiving grants under the residential substance abuse treatment program (42 U.S.C. 3796ff) to ensure that individuals participating in these programs receive aftercare services, including a full continuum of support services.

The act defines residential substance abuse treatment programs as a course of comprehensive individual and group substance abuse services lasting at least six months in residential treatment facilities that are set apart from the general population of a prison or jail. The act also requires the AG to study the use and effectiveness of the funds used to provide the required aftercare services.

Definition of Violent Offender for Drug Court Program (§103)

The act modifies the government's current drug court grant program, restricting the current definition of "violent offender" to individuals charged with or convicted for certain offenses that are punishable by a sentence of longer than one year (prior there was no minimum sentence length).[64]

The act requires all grantees under this program to adhere to this definition of "violent offender" within three years of the enactment of the act (i.e., April 9, 2011), and requires the secretary to publish regulations to this effect within 90 days of enactment.

Any drug court not adhering to this definition by April 9, 2011, would see their grant allocations reduced.

New Offender Reentry Grant Programs

Subtitle B creates a number of new targeted grant programs within the Department of Justice (DOJ) relating to the reintegration of offenders into the community.

State and Local Reentry Courts (§111)

This provision creates a new grant program within DOJ to fund reentry courts. Subject to the availability of appropriations, grants up to $500,000 are made available for state and local adult and juvenile court systems in order to establish and maintain reentry courts. These courts will be tasked with monitoring juvenile and adult offenders reentering into the community and providing them with a coordinated and comprehensive array of services, including housing assistance, education, job training, health services, and substance abuse treatment. In order to be eligible for funding, applicants have to demonstrate the need for their program; create a long-term strategy and detailed implementation plan; identify the government and community entities that would be coordinated by the project; and describe the methodology and outcome measures that would be used to evaluate the program. Additionally, applicants are required to submit annual reports to DOJ including a summary of the activities carried out with the grant and an assessment of whether these activities are meeting the needs identified in the grant application. The act authorizes $10 million for this program in FY2009 and FY2010. The total federal share of funding for these grants is limited to 50%; however, up to 50% of the state and local matching funds (i.e., 25% of the overall grant) could be fulfilled through in-kind contributions of goods or services.

Drug Treatment Alternative to Prison Programs (§112)

This provision creates a new grant program for state and local prosecutors to fund the development, implementation, and expansion of drug treatment programs that are alternatives to imprisonment. The programs require eligible offenders, after having received the consent of the prosecutor, to participate in comprehensive drug treatment programs in lieu of imprisonment. Criminal charges would be dismissed upon completion of the program. Offenders failing to successfully complete their treatment programs would serve their original sentence. In order to be eligible for these programs, the offender in question could not have had any prior felony use of force convictions or have been charged with or convicted of an offense involving a firearm, a dangerous weapon, or the use of force against another individual. The act authorizes $10 million for this program in FY2009 and FY2010. The total federal share of funding for these grants is limited to 50%; however, up to 50% of the state and local matching funds (i.e., 25% of the overall grant) could be fulfilled through in-kind contributions of goods or services.

Family Substance Abuse Treatment Alternatives to Incarceration Grants (§113)

This provision creates a new grant program to develop, implement, and expand the use of family-based substance abuse treatment programs as alternatives to incarceration for non-violent parent drug offenders. Among other things, the treatment is required to be clinically appropriate, comprehensive, and long-term and would be provided in a residential setting rather than an outpatient or a hospital setting. The program is required to include the implementation of graduated sanctions applied on the basis of the offender's accountability throughout the course of the program and the development of reentry plans for offenders. Offenders failing to complete the program are required to complete the sentence for the underlying crime involved. Grantees are required to submit annual reports to DOJ detailing the effectiveness of their programs using evidence-based data. Prison-based programs are required to locate their programs in an area separate from the general population, to create and support treatment plans for incarcerated parents, and to ensure continuity of care if participating offenders are transferred to a different facility. The act authorizes $10 million in FY2009 and in FY2010 for these grants; not less than 5% of this total is to be allocated to Indian Tribes.

Grants to Evaluate and Improve Educational Methods at Prisons, Jails, and Juvenile Facilities (§114)

This program authorizes the AG, subject to the availability of appropriations, to make grants to evaluate, identify, and improve programs that focus on providing educational and vocational programs for offenders by identifying and implementing best practices. Grantees are required to submit reports within 90 days of the last day of the final fiscal year of a grant detailing the progress that they have made. The act authorizes appropriations of $5 million for this program in FY2009 and FY2010.

Technology Careers Training Demonstration Grants

The act authorizes the AG to make grants to states, units of local governments, territories, and Indian Tribes to provide technology career training for prisoners. Grants may be awarded for programs that establish technology careers training programs for offenders during the three-year period prior to their release. Access to the Internet during the program will be restricted to ensure public safety. Grantees must submit a report to DOJ describing and assessing the program each fiscal year. The act authorizes $10 million for this program in FY2009 and FY2010.

New Drug-Treatment and Mentoring Grant Programs

Title II of P.L. 110-199 authorizes a series of new grant programs for drug-treatment and mentoring purposes. Subtitle A (§201) focuses on drug treatment programs, Subtitles B and C (§§211-214) focus on training and mentoring programs, and Subtitle C (§231) would create a federal offender reentry program at the Bureau of Prisons.

Offender Reentry Substance Abuse and Criminal Justice Collaboration Program (§201)

The act authorizes the AG to make grants to states, units of local governments, territories, and Indian Tribes in order to improve drug treatment programs in prisons and reduce the use of alcohol and other drugs by long-term abusers under correctional supervision. Grants may be used to continue or improve existing drug treatment programs, develop and implement programs for long-term substance abusers, provide addiction recovery support services, and establish pharmacological drug treatment services as part of any drug treatment program offered to prisoners.[65] Grant applicants are required to identify the entities that will be involved in providing the treatment, certify that this treatment has been developed in consultation with the Single State Authority for Substance Abuse,[66] certify that the treatment will be clinically appropriate and will provide comprehensive treatment, and describe how evidence-based strategies have been incorporated into the program, including the collection and analysis of data. The AG is required to submit a report to Congress detailing best practices relating to substance abuse treatment in prison and comprehensive treatment of long-term substance abusers by September 30, 2009. Another report on the drug treatment programs funded through this grant program is required by September 30, 2010. The act authorizes appropriations of $15 million for this program in both FY2009 and FY2010.

Mentoring Grants to Nonprofit Organizations (§211)

This provision would create a new grant program to provide mentoring and other transitional services for offenders being released into the community. Funding could be used for mentoring programs both in placement and during reentry, programs providing transition services during reentry, and programs providing training for "offender and victims issues." Priority would be given to applicants providing for the evaluation of their programs, using randomized control trials to the maximum extent feasible. Applicants would be required to identify and report on specific outcome performance measures related to the overall goal of reducing recidivism. The bills would authorize $15 million in FY2009 and in FY2010 for these grants.

Responsible Reintegration of Offenders (§212)

The act authorizes the Secretary of Labor to make grants to non-profit organizations to provide a wide array of mentoring, job training and job placement services, and other comprehensive transitional services. Grants may not be used to provide substance abuse treatment, mental health treatment, or housing services; however, grants can be used to coordinate with other entities providing these services. Applications for the program must identify the specific eligible area that will be served and the need for support in this area and describe the services that will be provided, the partnerships that have been established with the criminal justice system and housing authorities, and how other sources of funding will be leveraged to provide support services. In order to be eligible for funding, programs must be located in urbanized areas or clusters (as determined by the Bureau of the Census) that have a large number of prisoners returning to the community and high recidivism rates (however, no definitions for a large number of returning prisoners or high recidivism rates are provided). To be eligible for the program, offenders would be at least 18 years old, have no prior adult convictions or convictions for violent or sex-related offenses, and have been released from prison no more than 180 days before they begin participating in the grant program.[67] Not more than 15% of the grant may be used to pay for administrative costs. The act authorizes $20 million in appropriations for the Secretary of Labor to carry out this section in both FY2009 and FY2010; up to 4% of the appropriation may be used to provide technical assistance.

Bureau of Prisons Policies on Mentoring Contacts (§213)

This provision directs the Director of the Bureau of Prisons (BOP) at DOJ to adopt and implement a policy by July 9, 2009, to ensure that mentors working with incarcerated offenders are permitted to continue providing their services to the offender after their release from prison. The Director is required to submit a report to Congress concerning this policy's implementation by September 20, 2009.

Bureau of Prisons Policies on Chapel Library Material (§214)

The Director of the BOP is required to discontinue the Standardized Chapel Library project, or any other project that compiles, lists, or restricts prisoner access to materials provided by chapel libraries by May 9, 2008. Exceptions are made for materials that incite, promote, or suggest violence and materials prohibited by law.

Federal Prisoner Reentry Program (§231)

The act establishes a prisoner reentry program within the BOP. BOP is required to create a federal prisoner reentry strategy that will

- assess each prisoner's skill level at the beginning of their prison term (including academic, vocational, health, cognitive, interpersonal, daily living, and other related skills);
- create a skills development plan for prisoners to be carried out during their term of imprisonment;
- determine program assignments for prisoners based on the needs identified by the assessment;
- give priority to the reentry needs of high-risk populations, including sex-offenders, career criminals, and prisoners with mental health problems;
- coordinate and collaborate with other criminal justice, community-based, and faith-based organizations;
- collect information about a prisoner's family relationships and parental responsibilities; and
- provide incentives for prisoners to participate in skills development programs.

Incentives for prisoners to participate in skills development programs include allowing offenders to spend the maximum amount of time in community confinement facilities. Additionally, BOP is required to assist offenders in obtaining identification prior to their release.

The act modifies current law to include a number of new duties for the Director of BOP. These new duties include the establishment of prerelease planning procedures for all federal offenders that help prisoners apply for federal and state benefits prior to their release, and the establishment of reentry planning procedures to provide federal offenders with information in a number of reentry-related areas.

BOP is required to establish and implement a system that will allow it to quantitatively track progress in responding to the reentry needs of its inmates and to provide an annual report to the House and Senate Committees on the Judiciary concerning its progress.

An annual report is also required containing recidivism statistics for federal prisoners, including information concerning the relative recidivism rates of offenders participating in major inmate programs. After the initial report establishes a baseline recidivism rate for BOP ex-offenders, the act establishes 5- and 10-year goals of 2% and 5% reductions in this rate, respectively.

BOP is further required to ensure that the United States Probation and Pretrial Services System has medical information for inmates scheduled for release in order to create supervision plans that address the medical and mental health care needs of ex-offenders, and to ensure that each prisoner in community confinement has access to medical and mental health care.

In addition to the offender reentry program established above, the act also establishes two new programs within BOP:

- A pilot program within BOP to determine the effectiveness of allowing certain elderly, non-violent offenders to serve the remainder of their sentences on home detention. In order to be eligible for this program, offenders would have to be 65 years old or older and have never been convicted of a violent or sex-related crime or given a life-sentence, among other things.
- A program to provide satellite tracking of certain high-risk individuals after their release from prison, in conjunction with the use of graduated sanctions, the provision of reentry related services, and the involvement the offender's family, a victim advocate, and the victim. The act authorizes $5 million for this purpose in FY2009 and in FY2010.

Offender Reentry Research (§241)

The act allows, but does not direct, the National Institute of Justice to conduct research into offender reentry. This research may include a study identifying the number and characteristics of children with incarcerated parents and their likelihood of engaging in criminal activity, a study identifying mechanisms to compare recidivism rates between states, and a study on the characteristics of individuals released from prison who do not recidivate.

The act also allows, but does not direct, the Bureau of Justice Statistics to conduct research on offender reentry. This research may include an analysis of the populations that present unique reentry challenges, studies to determine the characteristics of individuals who return to prison (including which individuals pose the highest risk to the community), annual reports on the profile of the population leaving detention and entering the community, a national recidivism study every three years, and a study of post incarceration supervision (e.g., parole) violations.

Grants to Study Post-Incarceration Supervision Violations (§242)

This provision creates a new grant program to fund state studies aimed at improving data-collection on offenders who have their post-incarceration supervision revoked in order to better identify which individuals pose the greatest risk to the community. In order to receive funding, states have to certify that their program would collect "comprehensive and reliable data" and have to provide this data to the Bureau of Justice Statistics.

Addressing the Needs of Children of Incarcerated Parents (§243)

This provision directs the AG to collect data and develop best practices concerning the communication and coordination between state corrections and child welfare agencies, especially as they relate to the safety and support of children of incarcerated parents.

The best practices developed should include policies, procedures, and programs that could be used to safeguard the parent-child bond during incarceration and assist incarcerated parents in planning for the future and well being of their children.

Study of Effectiveness of Depot Naltrexone for Heroin Addiction (§244)

The act authorizes the AG, acting through the National Institute of Justice, to make grants to public and private research entities to evaluate the effectiveness of depot naltrexone for the treatment of heroin addiction. In order to be eligible for funding, research entities must demonstrate that they conduct research in a public or private institution of higher education, that they plan to work with parole or probation officers for offenders under court supervision, and that they will use randomized control trials to evaluate their programs.

Grantees are required to submit reports to DOJ describing and assessing the uses of their grant.

Authorization of Appropriations for Research (§245)

The act authorizes $10 million in both FY2009 and FY2010 to carry out the research programs authorized by §§241-244.

Clarification of Authority to Place Prisoner in Community Corrections (§251)

This provision would require the Director of the BOP to ensure, to the extent practicable, that prisoners within the federal correctional system spend up to a year at the end of their sentence focusing on their reentry into the community. As part of this practice, BOP would be authorized to transfer offenders to community correctional facilities or to home confinement (for the shorter of the last 10% or six months of their sentence). The provision would also give BOP the discretion to disregard a court's order that an offender serve part of his sentence in a community correctional facility.

Residential Drug Abuse Program in Federal Prisons (§252)

The act replaces the current definition of a residential drug abuse program with language defining such a program as a course of individual and group activities and treatment lasting at least six months in residential treatment facilities that are set apart from the general prison population. The act also stipulate that this treatment can include pharmacotherapies that extend beyond the six-month period.

Contracting for Services for Post-Conviction Supervision of Offenders (§253)

This provision would give the Director of the Administrative Office of the United States Courts the authority to enter into contracts with public and private agencies to monitor and provide a wide array of services to offenders in the community to promote their reintegration.

Extension of National Prison Rape Elimination Commission (§261)

The act extends the authorization for the National Prison Rape Elimination Commission[68] from three years to five years.

End Notes

[1] U.S. Department of Justice, Office of Justice Programs, "Reentry," available at http://www.reentry.gov/.

[2] Heather C. West and William J. Sabol, Prisoners in 2009, U.S. Department of Justice, Office of Justice Programs, Bureau of Justice Statistics, NCJ 231675, Washington, DC, December 2010, p. 4, http://bjs.ojp.usdoj.gov/content/pub/ pdf/p09.pdf.

[3] U.S. Department of Justice, Bureau of Justice Statistics, "Reentry Trends in the United States: Recidivism," available at http://www.ojp.usdoj.gov/bjs/reentry/recidivism.htm. Hereafter cited as "Reentry Trends."

[4] Wilkinson, Reginald A., Director of the Ohio Department of Rehabilitation and Correction, "Offender Reentry: A Storm Overdue," Paper Prepared for Third National Forum on Restorative Justice, March 2002, available at http://www.drc.state.oh.us/web/Articles/ article98.htm. Hereafter cited as "A Storm Overdue."

[5] U.S. Department of Justice, Bureau of Justice Statistics, "State Prison Expenditures 2001," NCJ202949, June 2004, available at http://www.ojp.usdoj.gov/bjs/pub/pdf/spe01.pdf.

[6] U.S. Department of Justice, Office of Justice Programs, "Learn About Reentry," available at http://www.reentry.gov/ learn.html. Hereafter cited as "Learn About Reentry."

[7] U.S. Government Accountability Office, "Prisoner Release: Trends and Information on Reintegration Programs," GAO-01-483, June 2001, pp. 19-25. Hereafter referred to as "GAO Prisoner Release Report."

[8] A Storm Overdue.

[9] Taxman, Faye et al., "Targeting for Reentry: Matching Needs and Services to Maximize Public Safety," National Criminal Justice Reference Service, March 25, 2002.

[10] GAO Prisoner Release Report, p. 5.

[11] While this is generally the case, jails on occasion can also include individuals sentenced to prison terms lasting less than one year (misdemeanors) and convicted felons in jurisdictions where the prisons are overpopulated.

[12] From a CRS interview with the Bureau of Justice Statistics, May 17, 2007.

[13] U.S. Department of Justice, Office of Justice Program, Bureau of Justice Statistics, Key Facts at a Glance: Incarceration Rate, 1980-2009, http://bjs.ojp.usdoj.gov/content/glance/ tables/incrttab.cfm.

[14] Reentry Trends.

[15] A determinate sentence is a fixed sentence, while an indeterminate sentence is typically expressed as a range (i.e., 5 to 10 years). For additional information on sentencing guidelines, please refer to CRS Report RL32766, Federal Sentencing Guidelines: Background, Legal Analysis, and Policy Options, by Lisa M. Seghetti and Alison M. Smith.

[16] U.S. Department of Justice, Bureau of Justice Statistics, Truth in Sentencing in State Prisons, NCJ170032, January 1999.

[17] For an expanded discussion of the varying definitions of recidivism, refer to Allen Beck, Recidivism: A Fruit Salad Concept in the Criminal Justice World, Justice Concepts, available at http://www.justiceconcepts.com/recidivism.pdf.

[18] See Colorado Department of Corrections, Recidivism and Cumulative Return Rates: Calendar Year Releases from 1999 through 2005, available at http://www.doc.state.co.us/Statistics/pdfs/Recidivism/2007RecidBulletin.pdf.

[19] See Florida Department of Corrections, Recidivism Report: Inmates Released from Florida Prisons, May 2001, available at http://www.dc.state.fl.us/pub/recidivism/2001/full.pdf.

[20] Patrick A. Langan and David J. Levin, United States Department of Justice, Bureau of Justice Statistics, Recidivism of Prisoners Released in 1994, Report NCJ193427, June 2002. Hereafter referred to as "1994 Recidivism Study."

[21] The states included in the study were Arizona, California, Delaware, Florida, Illinois, Maryland, Michigan, Minnesota, New Jersey, New York, North Carolina, Ohio, Oregon, Texas, and Virginia.

[22] 1994 Recidivism Study, p. 7.

[23] Pew Center on the States, State of Recidivism: The Revolving Door of America's Prisons, Washington, DC, April 2011, http://www.pewtrusts.org/uploadedFiles/wwwpewtrustsorg/Reports/sentencing_and_corrections/State_Recidivism_Revolving_Door_America_Prisons%20.pdf.

[24] Recidivism was defined as a return to prison, either for being convicted for a new crime or violating the terms of post-incarceration supervision. Ibid., p. 7.

[25] Pew notes that the high number of releases and rate of return for offenders from California has a significant effect on national recidivism rates, hence California was excluded from the comparison of recidivism rate for states that were included in both the BJS and Pew studies. Ibid., p. 12.

[26] United States Sentencing Commission, A Comparison of the Federal Sentencing Guidelines Criminal History Category and the U.S. Parole Commission Salient Factor Score.

[27] For examples of how the CHC system works within the federal sentencing guidelines, please refer to CRS Report RL32846, How the Federal Sentencing Guidelines Work: Two Examples, by Charles Doyle.

[28] Joan Petersilla, "What Works in Prisoner Reentry? Reviewing and Questioning the Evidence," Federal Probation, vol. 68, no. 2, 2004, pp. 4-8. Hereafter referred to as "Questioning the Evidence."

[29] Drug court programs typically divert nonviolent offenders arrested for drug-related crimes to treatment centers as opposed to prison.

[30] Questioning the Evidence, p. 7.

[31] Richard P. Seiter and Karen R. Kadela, "Prisoner Reentry: What Works, What Does Not, and What Is Promising," Crime & Delinquency, vol. 49, no. 3, 2003, pp. 360-388. Hereafter referred to as "Prisoner Reentry: What Works."

[32] Questioning the Evidence, 4-5.

[33] Questioning the Evidence, p. 5.

[34] Prisoner Reentry: What Works, p. 370.

[35] Meta-analyses are a type of systematic review of studies that allow researchers to draw conclusions across a wide range of studies by using statistical methods to derive quantitative results from the analysis of multiple sources of quantitative evidence.

[36] Lawrence W. Sherman, Denise Gottfredson, Doris MacKenzie, John Eck, Peter Reuter, and Shawn Bushway, Preventing Crime: What Works, What Doesn't, What's Promising, National Institute of Justice, 1997.

[37] Offender Reentry: What Works.

[38] Offender Reentry: What Works, pp. 370-373.

[39] See, for example, Shawn Bushway and Peter Reuter, "Labor Markets and Crime Risk Factors," in Preventing Crime: What Works, What Doesn't, What's Promising. A Report to the United States Congress, the National Institute of Justice, 1997, Chapter 6. Jeremy Travis, But They All Come Back: Facing the Challenges of Prisoner Reentry, The Urban Institute Press, 2005.

[40] Prisoner Reentry: What Works, pp. 373-374.

[41] Prisoner Reentry: What Works, p. 374.

[42] Prisoner Reentry: What Works, p. 378. A study's statistical significance is typically interpreted as a level of confidence (usually expressed as a probability, e.g., 95%) that an estimated impact is not merely the result of random variation, indicating that at least some of the measured impact may, with substantial confidence (e.g., 95% confidence), be attributed to the treatment as a cause.

[43] Prisoner Reentry: What Works, pp. 376-379.

[44] For more information about the use of randomized control trials to evaluate government programs, refer to CRS Report RL33301, Congress and Program Evaluation: An Overview of Randomized Controlled Trials (RCTs) and Related Issues, by Clinton T. Brass, Erin D. Williams, and Blas Nuñez-Neto.

[45] Questioning the Evidence, p. 7.

[46] Questioning the Evidence, pp. 6-7.

[47] U.S. Department of Justice, Office of Justice Programs, 2005 Congressional Budget Justifications, p. 37.

[48] Pamela K. Lattimore and Christy A. Visher, The Multi-site Evaluation of SVORI: Summary and Synthesis, RTI International, December 2009, http://svori.rti.org/documents/reports/SVORI_Summary_Synthesis_FINAL.pdf.

[49] The evaluation included a pre-release interview (conducted approximately 30 day before being released) with both SVORI and non-SVORI participants. Follow-up interviews were conducted 3, 9, and 15 months after release. In addition, oral swab drug tests were conducted during the 3 and 15 month interviews. Recidivism data was collected from the Federal Bureau of Investigation's National Crime Information Center (NCIC) and state correctional and juvenile justice agencies. Ibid., p. ES-7.

[50] A more detailed description of the Second Chance Act can be found in the Appendix.

[51] U.S. Department of Labor, Employment & Training Administration, "Serious and Violent Offender Reentry Initiative Appendices," available at http://www.doleta.gov/sga/sga/reentry_app.cfm.

[52] For more information about the Workforce Investment Act, please refer to CRS Report RL33687, The Workforce Investment Act (WIA): Program-by-Program Overview and Funding of Title I Training Programs, by David H. Bradley.

[53] For more information about the Work Opportunity Tax Credits Program, please refer to CRS Report RL30089, The Work Opportunity Tax Credit (WOTC), by Christine Scott.

[54] U.S. Department of Labor, Employment & Training Administration, "Work Opportunity Tax Credit" available at http://www.doleta.gov/business/Incentives/opptax/.

[55] For more information about the Federal Bonding Program, please refer to CRS Report RL30248, The Employment Service: The Federal-State Public Labor Exchange System, by Alison Pasternak and Ann Lordeman.

[56] U.S. Department of Labor, Employment & Training Administration, "Federal Bonding Program," available at http://www.bonds4jobs.com/program-background.html.

[57] U.S. Department of Education, "Life Skills for State and Local Prisoners Program," available at http://www.ed.gov/ programs/lifeskills/index.html.

[58] U.S. Department of Education, "Guide to U.S. Department of Education Programs, FY2007," p. 38, available at http://www.ed.gov/programs/gtep/gtep.pdf.

[59] U.S. Department of Labor, Employment & Training Administration, "Serious and Violent Offender Reentry Initiative Appendices," available at http://www.doleta.gov/sga/sga/reentry_app.cfm.

[60] U.S. Department of Labor, Employment & Training Administration, "Serious and Violent Offender Reentry Initiative Appendices," available at http://www.doleta.gov/ sga/sga/reentry_app.cfm.

[61] For more information about SAMHSA, please refer to CRS Report RL33997, Substance Abuse and Mental Health Services Administration (SAMHSA): Reauthorization Issues, by Ramya Sundararaman.

[62] Testimony of Senior Policy Advisor to the Administrator Cheri Nolan, Substance Abuse and Mental Health Services Administration, U.S. Department of Health and Human Services, before the Committee on the Judiciary, Subcommittee on Corrections and Rehabilitation, Thursday, September 21, 2006.

[63] U.S. Department of Labor, Employment & Training Administration, "Serious and Violent Offender Reentry Initiative Appendices," available at http://www.doleta.gov/ sga/sga/reentry_app.cfm.

[64] In order to be considered a "violent offender," an individual has to have committed this crime while in possession of a firearm or dangerous weapon, the crime has to have resulted in the death or serious bodily injury of a person, force had to have been used against someone's person, or the offender had 1 or more prior convictions for a felony crime of violence involving the use or attempted use of force against a person with the intent to cause death or serious bodily harm. See 42 U.S.C. 3797 u-2(a)(1).

[65] Pharmacological drug treatment involves using drugs and medications in the treatment of substance abuse. See Clayton Mosher, Scott Akins, and Chad Smith, "Pharmacological Drug Treatment" Paper presented at the annual meeting of the American Society of Criminology, Royal York, Toronto. 2008-04-21.

[66] States would be required to identify an entity that would be the single State administrative authority responsible for planning, developing, implementing, monitoring, regulating, and evaluating substance abuse services within the State.

[67] Grantees may exempt 10% of their clients from this 180-day requirement.

[68] 42 U.S.C. 15606(d)(3)(A).

In: Inmate Release, Reintegration and Reentry ISBN: 978-1-62417-996-9
Editor: Chris Homesley

Chapter 2

INMATE REENTRY PROGRAMS: ENHANCED INFORMATION SHARING COULD FURTHER STRENGTHEN COORDINATION AND GRANT MANAGEMENT*

United States Government Accountability Office

ABBREVIATIONS

BOP	Federal Bureau of Prisons
CFDA	Catalog of Federal Domestic Assistance
DOJ	Department of Justice
GMS	Grants Management System
HHS	Department of Health and Human Services
MIS	Management Information System
PMT	Performance Measurement Tool
PRI	Prisoner Reentry Initiative
ORP	Offender Reentry Program
RExO	Reintegration of Ex-Offenders
SAIS	Service Accountability Improvement System
SCA	Second Chance Act

* This is an edited, reformatted and augmented version of The United States Government Accountability Office publication, Report to Congressional Committees, GAO-13-93, dated December 2012.

SVORI Serious and Violent Offender Reentry Initiative

WHY GAO DID THIS STUDY

About 700,000 inmates are released from federal and state custody each year, and another 9 million are booked into and released from local jails. Former inmates face challenges as they transition into, or reenter, society, such as finding housing and employment. According to the most recent data available, more than two-thirds of state prisoners are rearrested for a new offense within 3 years of release, and about half are reincarcerated. Federal reentry grants are available for state and local providers, as successful reentry reduces rearrest or reincarceration, known as recidivism. GAO was asked to review (1) the extent to which there is fragmentation, overlap, and duplication across federal reentry grant programs; (2) the coordination efforts federal grant-making agencies have taken to prevent unnecessary duplication and share promising practices; and (3) the extent to which federal grant-making agencies measure grantees' effectiveness in reducing recidivism. GAO identified and analyzed the grant programs and agencies that supported reentry efforts in fiscal year 2011; analyzed agency documents, such as grant solicitations; and interviewed agency officials.

WHAT GAO RECOMMENDS

GAO recommends that DOJ, Labor, and HHS enhance their information sharing on approaches for determining how effectively grantees reduce recidivism. In response, DOJ, Labor, and HHS reported that they would take actions to address our recommendation.

WHAT GAO FOUND

In fiscal year 2011, the Departments of Justice (DOJ), Labor (Labor), and Health and Human Services (HHS) separately administered nine fragmented but minimally overlapping reentry grant programs with low risk of duplication. Specifically, GAO found that these grant programs are fragmented since more than one federal agency is involved in administering the programs. Further, GAO found that overlap across the nine programs was minimal because the programs varied in (1) their applicant eligibility criteria, (2) the extent to which their funds solely benefit the reentry population, and (3) their primary services funded. For example, Labor's reentry program limits eligibility to private, nonprofit organizations that will use the funds primarily to assist current or former inmates—residing in or released from any facility—with their employment needs. In contrast, one of DOJ's reentry programs limits eligibility to governmental entities that will use the funds primarily to assist current or former inmates— residing in or released from state, local, or tribal facilities—with their substance abuse treatment needs. Given the variance across eligible applicants, beneficiaries, and primary services, the overlap across the nine programs is minimal and the risk of duplication—when two or more agencies or programs are engaged in the same activities, provide the same services to the same beneficiaries, or provide funding for the same purpose—is low.

DOJ, Labor, and HHS have acknowledged where some overlap exists and therefore have taken steps to coordinate their reentry efforts to further prevent unnecessary duplication and share promising practices. For example, in 2011, the U.S. Attorney General convened the Federal Interagency Reentry Council—a group of federal agencies whose mission is to make communities safer; assist those returning from prison and jail in becoming productive, taxpaying citizens; and save taxpayer dollars by lowering the direct and collateral costs of incarceration. Further, agency officials from all three agencies reported that they share grant solicitations with one another before issuing them, and in 2009, DOJ and HHS established a memorandum of agreement to formally coordinate funding activities related to reentry. In addition, all three agencies have taken action, or have actions under way, to require their grant applicants to report other federal funds they are receiving, or plan to receive, and consider this information before they will make new award decisions.

DOJ, Labor, and HHS are measuring grantee performance and conducting program evaluations, but they could enhance information sharing about the methods they use to collect and analyze data to determine how effectively grantees reduce recidivism. To monitor grantee performance, DOJ, Labor, and HHS collect different performance information, such as rearrest, reincarceration, and employment rates, through several web-based grant management systems, each with varying strengths and limitations. However, the agencies have not formally discussed these systems with one another, or how they analyze the data they collect, despite engaging in collaborations during which such discussions would be practical and useful. Consistent with effective interagency coordination practices, sharing information like this could help the agencies better leverage existing practices and improve their approaches to determining and reporting on grantee effectiveness.

December 14, 2012

The Honorable Lamar Smith
Chairman

The Honorable John Conyers, Jr.
Ranking Member
Committee on the Judiciary
House of Representatives

The Honorable F. James Sensenbrenner, Jr.
Chairman

The Honorable Robert C. "Bobby" Scott
Ranking Member
Subcommittee on Crime, Terrorism, and Homeland Security
Committee on the Judiciary
House of Representatives

About 2.2 million individuals were incarcerated in state, federal, and local facilities in 2011, and the United States spent more than an estimated $82.7 billion on federal, state, and local corrections, according to the most recently available data.[1] About 700,000 inmates are released from federal and state custody each year, and another 9 million are booked into and released from local jails. These former inmates face considerable challenges as they transition into, or reenter, society after incarceration. When successful reentry fails, rearrest or reincarceration may result. According to the most recent data available, more than two-thirds of state prisoners are rearrested for a new offense within 3 years of their release and about half are reincarcerated—this is known as recidivism.[2] Assisting the reentry population—former inmates or inmates preparing for release from federal, state, and local correctional facilities—in successful reentry is essential, as the economic and societal costs of high incarceration rates are significant. High rates of recidivism mean more crime, more victims, and more pressure on an already overburdened and overcrowded criminal justice system. As we have recently reported, inmate crowding remains a significant concern, and federal prisons are nearly 40 percent over capacity.[3]

In 2011, the U.S. Attorney General convened the Federal Interagency Reentry Council—a group of federal agencies whose mission is to make communities safer; assist those returning from prison and jail in becoming productive, taxpaying citizens; and save taxpayer dollars by lowering the direct and collateral costs of incarceration.[4] Unlike some other executive branch councils, the Federal Interagency Reentry Council does not receive an appropriation from Congress and does not employ full-time staff.[5] Member agencies provide a range of services, from direct assistance with reentry to the administration of grants. For example, the Department of Justice's (DOJ) Federal Bureau of Prisons (BOP) is the sole agency responsible for the custody of more than 218,000 federal inmates, and considers the process of reentry to begin the day the inmate is incarcerated. Accordingly, BOP is involved in the direct provision of reentry services, such as vocational training, faith-based programs, and substance abuse treatment, which help current inmates prepare for release. For fiscal year 2012, BOP estimates spending about 9 percent, or $604 million of its $6.6 billion operating budget, on reentry-related services. In contrast, DOJ's Bureau of Justice Assistance and the Departments of Labor (Labor) and Health and Human Services (HHS) all administer grant funding to state and local reentry service providers so that they may, for example, assist the reentry population train for and find jobs, obtain substance abuse treatment, and locate housing as needed. Collectively, these three federal agencies were appropriated over $165 million in fiscal year 2012 and nearly $185 million in fiscal year 2011 for three of their respective reentry grant programs. These three funding streams—the Second Chance Act (SCA) program, the Reintegration of Ex-Offenders (RExO) program, and the Offender Reentry Program (ORP)—support both the adult and the juvenile reentry population.[6]

We have previously reported on the importance of sound federal grant management practices.[7] We have also published annual reports on fragmentation, overlap, and duplication across the government since 2011, emphasizing opportunities to achieve greater efficiencies and more effective delivery of government services,[8] and have studied grants management at DOJ in particular.[9] In 2012, we reported that DOJ's grant programs overlap across 10 justice areas, contributing to the risk of unnecessarily duplicative grant awards for the same or similar purposes.[10] Moreover, the DOJ, Labor, and HHS Inspectors General have listed grant management or grant accountability among their respective departments' top 10 management challenges from at least 2007 through 2011. The DOJ Inspector General has also included detention and incarceration on its list since 2006.

Given the importance of inmate rehabilitation and the variety of federal initiatives, including grants, to facilitate successful reentry, you asked us to review the role various federal agencies play in helping to reduce recidivism, and what agencies know about the effectiveness of the programs they administer. Specifically, this report addresses the following questions (1) To what extent is there fragmentation across the federal grant programs that exist to support inmates' reentry into society, and to what extent do these grant programs overlap or duplicate? (2) What coordination efforts have federal grant-making agencies taken, if any, to prevent unnecessary duplication and share information on promising reentry approaches? (3) To what extent do federal grant-making agencies measure grantees' effectiveness in reducing recidivism?

Using the framework established in our prior work addressing overlap, fragmentation, and duplication, we use the following definitions for analysis of reentry grant programs:

- Fragmentation: when more than one federal agency (or more than one organization within an agency) is involved in the same broad area of national interest.
- Overlap: when programs have similar goals, devise similar strategies and activities to achieve those goals, or target similar users. Overlap may result from statutory or other limitations beyond an agency's control.
- Duplication: when two or more agencies or programs are engaged in the same activities or provide the same services to the same beneficiaries. When granting agencies do not identify overlap, assess its impact, or coordinate their activities in acknowledgment of the overlap, there is a heightened risk of unnecessary duplication because one granting agency may not be knowledgeable of the ways in which its funding decision duplicates another's. At times, federal funding is leveraged by design to achieve a single purpose through multiple federal funding streams. These funding arrangements are not characterized as unnecessary duplication for purposes of this review so long as federal agencies are aware of them and have deliberately planned for grant programs to be complementary. Duplication also

occurs when a single grantee uses grant funds from different federal sources to pay for the exact same expenditure.

To address our first and second objectives, we first identified federal grant programs that supported reentry efforts in fiscal year 2011. Specifically, we identified grant programs that provided either new or continuation funds to support direct services for the adult reentry population. In order to be included in our scope, the grant program—or a grant solicitation under this program—must have either (1) specifically targeted the reentry population for its services, included the reentry population as a target population, or (2) included an element specific to reentry or corrections for which the funding could be used. We identified the grant programs meeting these criteria through key word searches in federal databases— the Catalog of Federal Domestic Assistance (CFDA), Grants.gov, and USASpending.gov—as well as a review of agency documents.[11] We excluded programs that did not meet all our criteria, including programs that the reentry population may benefit from but are not specifically targeted. Utilizing the framework established in our prior work addressing fragmentation, overlap, and duplication, we then reviewed the grant solicitations issued under these grant programs to make determinations about the extent to which they were fragmented, overlapping, or duplicative.[12] In making these determinations, we considered, collectively, three factors: (1) which applicants were eligible for the grant programs, (2) the extent to which the reentry population is the sole target of the grant programs' services, and (3) the primary services these grant programs funded. Further, we interviewed agency officials from DOJ, Labor, and HHS to gauge their awareness of other federal reentry funds and where they were being allocated. We also interviewed officials from the Council of State Governments Justice Center and the Association of State Correctional Administrators, and examined a number of federal agency and industry reports on the services needed to ensure effective reentry.[13] To determine how agencies coordinate with one another in the administration of these programs, we reviewed agency documents, such as a memorandum of understanding between DOJ and HHS, and Federal Interagency Reentry Council reports, such as the 2011 Reentry Council Accomplishment Report. In addition, we conducted interviews with officials from DOJ, Labor, and HHS, as well as the Federal Interagency Reentry Council to obtain a better understanding of what grant programs they operate and how they coordinate with one another.[14] We compared agencies' coordination activities with best practices for interagency collaborations.[15] Further, we conducted visits to three states—New York, California, and Texas.

We selected these three states based on the size of each state's inmate population and the concentration of reentry grants provided in 2011 within their specific jurisdictions. We interviewed nine grantees in these states because they were located in jurisdictions that received multiple grants. While we cannot generalize the results of our interviews with these grantees to all grantees, we were able to obtain more specific information on the types of services funded with federal grants funds and the grantees' views on coordination activities.

To add additional context to our audit work, during our visits to California and Texas, we also met with officials in nearby BOP facilities to discuss their reentry efforts. Our observations from these visits cannot be generalized, but our discussions with the BOP officials illuminated the challenges with which inmates are faced upon their release and the reentry programs specific prisons are providing while inmates are in their custody.

To analyze the extent to which DOJ, Labor, and HHS use grant monitoring and assessments to determine program effectiveness in reducing recidivism, we analyzed agency documentation, such as 2011 grant solicitations that outline grantee reporting requirements, grant management policy guidance, and the agencies' most recently available reports on grant program evaluations.

We also interviewed officials from DOJ, Labor, and HHS to learn more about their grant-monitoring and evaluation practices, as well as their grant management systems. We reviewed guidance to federal agencies from the GPRA Modernization Act of 2010 and best practices for interagency collaborations.[16]

Further, during our visits, we asked grantees about their experiences in collecting recidivism data and providing performance information to the federal agencies that funded them. We also analyzed these grantees' most recent quarterly performance reports—reports that grantees are required to submit to their federal granting agency describing the ways in which they have used the grant funds and their specific accomplishments.

We conducted this performance audit from January 2012 through December 2012 in accordance with generally accepted government auditing standards.

Those standards require that we plan and perform the audit to obtain sufficient, appropriate evidence to provide a reasonable basis for our findings and conclusions based on our audit objectives. We believe that the evidence obtained provides a reasonable basis for our findings and conclusions based on our audit objectives.

BACKGROUND

Reentry Population Needs

The potential needs of the reentry population vary and generally cross over several areas, as shown in figure 1. For example, according to the BOP Director's statement to Congress in March 2012, most inmates need assistance with things such as job skills, vocational training, education, substance abuse treatment, and parenting skills if they are to successfully reenter society.[17] Further, according to the Federal Interagency Reentry Council, about 66 percent of inmates have substance abuse or dependence issues, and 24 percent have mental illness issues. In addition, according to various Urban Institute reports on reentry, between 54 and 40 percent of former inmates were not able to obtain employment within 7 to 10 months of release.[18] In addition, former inmates are subject to a wide variety of legal and regulatory sanctions and restrictions, which are referred to as collateral consequences.[19]

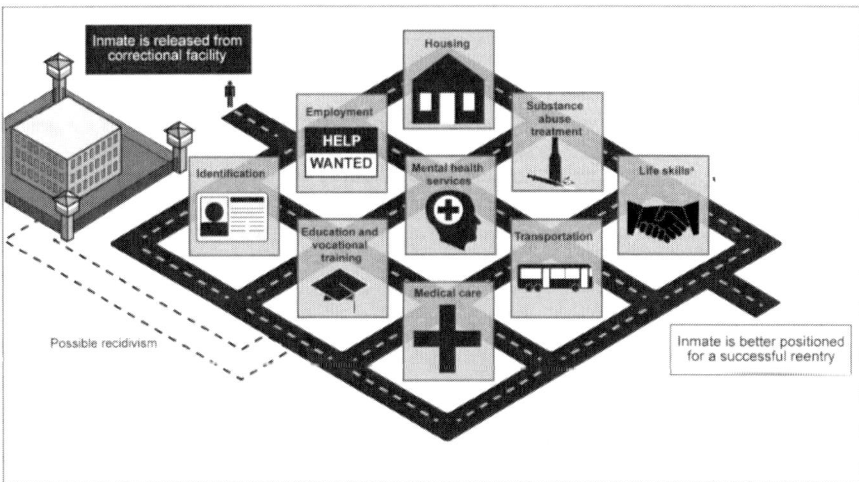

Source: GAO Art Explosion. (graphics)

[a] Life skills services are provided through mentoring and counseling and address issues such as parenting and behavioral/anger management.

Figure 1. Potential Needs of the Reentry Population.

BOP provides reentry services to inmates within federal prisons (see app. I for a list of services). Other federal agencies, through their reentry grant program funds, assist state and local entities in providing reentry services to the reentry population that may return to their communities.[20] For example, a community nonprofit organization may receive a federal grant to assist members of the reentry population in their job training skills following inmates' release from prison. Such services funded through the grant may include job placement or vocational training, such as construction.

Grant Program Administration and Reentry Grant History

Federal grant programs are generally created by statute and funded through appropriations. Competitive grants are announced through solicitations—or announcements to applicants of funding opportunities— and a single program may award funding through multiple solicitations. Once a grant is awarded, statutes may require that a primary grant recipient—that is, the one to whom the federal agency makes the original award—then award a portion of its grant to a subgrantee. Where statutes do not require subgranting, a grantee may voluntarily choose to award all or a portion of its funds to subgrantees. Further, federal agencies' monitoring of grantee performance is important to help ensure that grantees are meeting program and accountability requirements. Table 1 describes the phases of the federal grant life cycle and the common activities agencies engage in within each phase.

Table 1. Four Phases of the Federal Grant Life Cycle

Grant phase	Common activities
Preaward	• Announce the opportunity • Receive and review applications
Award	• Notify the grantee • Publicly announce the awarding of funds
Implementation	• Disburse payment • Collect and review grantee progress reports • Conduct site visits to monitor for compliance
Closeout	• Reconcile financial data and other reports

Source: GAO.

Federal grants to assist with reentry efforts have been in place for several years and have had a number of incarnations. Two of these former efforts are the Serious and Violent Offender Reentry Initiative (SVORI) and the Prisoner Reentry Initiative (PRI).[21] SVORI—a $300 million collaborative effort among

DOJ, Labor, HHS, and the Departments of Education and Housing and Urban Development—began in 2002. The goal of the SVORI grant program was to reduce recidivism among high-risk offenders—those who faced multiple challenges upon returning to the community from incarceration. SVORI concluded in fiscal year 2005, but its goals continued through the PRI, which DOJ and Labor administered. The PRI grant program focused on reducing recidivism by helping former inmates find work and providing them access to other critical services in their communities. PRI concluded in fiscal year 2008 when its appropriation expired.

Since PRI's conclusion, DOJ, Labor, and HHS each have implemented grant programs that support reentry services at the state and local levels. The Second Chance Act of 2007 authorizes the Attorney General to administer federal grants to state and local government agencies, territories, or Indian tribes, or any combination thereof, in partnership with stakeholders, service providers, and nonprofit organizations to provide employment assistance, substance abuse treatment, housing, mentoring, and other services that can help reduce recidivism.[22] DOJ administers these grants through the SCA program and has awarded funding through a number of SCA solicitations.[23] Under the Second Chance Act of 2007 and the Workforce Investment Act of 1998, Labor implemented its RExO program and has awarded funding through a few RExO solicitations.[24] RExO is designed to strengthen communities to which the majority of former inmates return to through an employment-centered program that incorporates mentoring, job training, and other comprehensive transitional services. This program seeks to reduce recidivism by helping former inmates find work when they return to their communities. Finally, HHS developed the ORP solicitation under its Programs of Regional and National Significance grant program.[25] The purpose of ORP is to expand or enhance substance abuse treatment and related recovery and reentry services to former inmates returning to the community.

Prior Findings Related to Fragmentation, Overlap, and Duplication across DOJ Grant Programs

In 2010, we were directed to identify programs, agencies, offices, and initiatives with duplicative goals and activities within departments and government-wide and report annually to Congress.[26] In March 2011 and February 2012, we issued our first two annual reports in response to this requirement.[27] In our 2012 report and a subsequent follow-on report, we found that of the 253 grant solicitations that DOJ issued in fiscal year 2010, there was overlap across 10 justice areas, including corrections, recidivism, and reentry. We reported that this overlap contributed to the risk of unnecessarily duplicative grant awards for the same or similar purposes.[28] We also reported that DOJ generally lacked awareness of the extent to which its grant programs overlapped and thus was not positioned to minimize the risk of potential unnecessary duplication before making grant awards. In the July 2012 report that expanded on these findings, we recommended, among other things, that DOJ assess its grant programs for overlap and that DOJ require its grant applicants to report past, current, and prospective federal funding it has or plans to receive.[29] DOJ agreed with our recommendations and has begun to take steps to implement them, such as exploring options to carry out an assessment to determine the extent of unnecessary duplication, if any, and the risk associated with unnecessary program duplication.

Federal Reentry Grant Programs Are Fragmented but Minimally Overlapping, Reducing the Risk for Duplication

Nine Reentry Grant Programs Are Fragmented across Three Federal Agencies

DOJ, Labor, and HHS separately provided new or continuation grant funding to support direct services to the adult reentry population through nine grant programs in fiscal year 2011. Since more than one federal agency is involved in this same broad area of national interest, these programs are fragmented. As shown in table 2, these agencies awarded about $630 million to new grantees in that year.[30] In some cases, the program is exclusively for reentry—as is the case with Labor's RExO program. In other instances, such as DOJ's Edward Byrne Memorial Justice Assistance Grant program, grantees may use the money for reentry-related services, but they may also use it for other criminal justice-related matters, such as indigent defense.[31]

Fragmentation of these federal grant programs is due in part to the legislative creation of the programs.

For example, under the Second Chance Act of 2007, DOJ is directed to administer federal grants to provide employment assistance, substance abuse treatment, housing, mentoring, and other services that can help reduce recidivism.[32]

Accordingly, DOJ developed the SCA grant program, and issued a variety of solicitations under this grant program.

While HHS is required to address priority substance abuse treatment needs of regional and national significance, the Secretary may carry out these activities directly or through grants or cooperative agreements, and accordingly, HHS developed the ORP solicitation.[33]

Table 2. Fragmentation across Federal Reentry Grant Programs in Fiscal Year 2011

Department/ agency	Grant program	Number of new grantees	Funding awarded to new grantees	Number of new grantees specific to reentry	Funding for new grantees specific for reentry
Justice/Bureau of Justice Assistance	Second Chance Act	99	$40,983,248	99	$40,983,248
	Residential Substance Abuse Treatment for State Prisoners	55	$22,817,755	N/A[a]	
	Edward Byrne Memorial Justice Assistance Grant	56	$246,018,352	N/A[a]	
	Justice and Mental Health Collaboration	40	$7,757,426	N/A[a]	
Labor/ Employment and Training Administration	Reintegration of Ex-Offenders	25b	$30,227,870	25	$30,227,870
Health and Human Services/ Various Agencies	Programs of Regional and National Significance (includes the Offender Reentry Program) (Agency: Substance Abuse and Mental Health Services Administration)	262	$160,854,143	N/A[c]	

Table 2. (Continued)

Department/ agency	Grant program	Number of new grantees	Funding awarded to new grantees	Number of new grantees specific to reentry	Funding for new grantees specific for reentry
	Healthy Marriage Promotion and Responsible Fatherhood Grants (Agency: Administration for Children and Families)	134[d]	$121,393,729	5	$6,744,690
	The Linkage to Life Program: Rebuilding Broken Bridges for Minority Families Impacted by HIV/AIDS (Agency: Office of the Secretary)	N/A[e]			
	Health Improvement for Re-entering Ex-offenders Initiative (Agency: Office of the Secretary)	N/A[f]			

Source: GAO analysis of information obtained from DOJ, Labor, and HHS.

[a] Not applicable; according to DOJ officials, they are not able to separate out grant funds provided for reentry-related services.

[b] Department of Labor Reintegration of Ex-Offenders funds are awarded on a program-year basis.

[c] Not applicable; no new grants were awarded in fiscal year 2011, only continuation funding was provided in this year. HHS provided continuation funds totaling $16,373,000 to 41 grantees.

[d] This includes 14 child welfare grants issued under this grant program.

[e] Not applicable; no new grants were awarded in fiscal year 2011, only continuation funding was provided in this year. HHS provided continuation funds totaling $2,840,000 to six grantees. According to HHS officials, all six grantees provide services to the reentry population, as well as other target populations. However, the funds cannot be separated out by target population.

[f] Not applicable; no new grants were awarded in fiscal year 2011, only continuation funding was provided in this year. HHS provided continuation funds totaling $1,977,511 to eight grantees—all that provide services to the reentry population.

Grant Program Overlap Is Minimal and the Risk of Duplication Is Low

When considering, collectively, which applicants are eligible for the grant programs, the extent to which the reentry population is the sole target of the grant programs' services, and the primary services these grant programs fund, we found that overlap across the nine programs was minimal. Therefore, the risk of duplication—when two or more agencies or programs are engaged in the same activities, provide the same services to the same beneficiaries, or provide funding for the same purpose—is low.

With respect to applicant eligibility, because there are three primary categories of applicants—state and local governments; tribal governments; and private, nonprofit, and community-based organizations—there is some overlap in this area.

Specifically, as illustrated in table 3, five of the nine grant programs extended eligibility to all three categories of applicants.[34]

However, one allowed only state and local government applicants, and another allowed only private, nonprofit, or community-based applicants. Analyzing the data from the vantage point of the applicants themselves, state and local government agencies could apply to eight of the nine programs; tribal governments could apply to seven; and private, nonprofit, or community-based could apply to six.

Nevertheless, with respect to the extent to which the grant programs targeted the reentry grant population, we found greater variation and less overlap.

Across the nine programs, as table 4 illustrates, three restricted, or targeted, their funds exclusively for use in assisting the reentry population. These were DOJ's SCA program, Labor's RExO program, and HHS's Health Improvement for Re-entering Ex-offenders Initiative. Another five programs offered a range of solicitations, but at least one of these programs' solicitations exclusively targeted the reentry population. For example, HHS issued a solicitation for ORP under its Programs of Regional and National Significance Program.

Last, one program—DOJ's Edward Byrne Memorial Justice Assistance Grant Program—was so broad as to encompass reentry amongst a number of other criminal justice or corrections uses. Since more than half of the programs target populations other than the reentry population, the overlap in this area is minimal.

Table 3. Variations in Applicant Eligibility across Federal Reentry Grant Programs, Fiscal Year 2011

Department	Grant program		Eligible entity	
		Governmental agencies (state, local)	Tribal government	Private, nonprofit, or community-based organizations
Justice	Second Chance Act	X	X	X[a]
	Residential Substance Abuse Treatment for State Prisoners	X		
	Edward Byrne Memorial Justice Assistance Grant	X	X	
	Justice and Mental Health Collaboration	X	X	
Labor	Reintegration of Ex-Offenders			X
Health and Human Services	Programs of Regional and National Significance (includes the Offender Reentry Program)	X	X	X
	Healthy Marriage Promotion and Responsible Fatherhood Grants	X	X	X
	The Linkage to Life Program: Rebuilding Broken Bridges for Minority Families Impacted by HIV/AIDS	X	X	X
	Health Improvement for Re-entering Ex-offenders Initiative	X	X	X

Source: GAO analysis of grant solicitations.

[a] Only one of the eight grant solicitations issued in fiscal year 2011 for adult former inmates under the Second Chance Act was open to nongovernmental agencies.

We also found greater variation, and thus less overlap, when assessing the primary services these nine grant programs fund, as shown in table 5. Across the nine programs, one grant program covered a wide range of reentry services; two programs' primary services were mental health and substance abuse; one program's primary services were employment and life, family, and parenting skills; and the remaining five programs had one or no primary use of funding. For example, DOJ's Residential Substance Abuse Treatment for State Prisoners primarily funded substance abuse treatment for state prisoners, and Labor's RExO program primarily funded services for employment assistance.

Analyzing the data from the vantage point of the primary services, the greatest number of programs—four of the nine—focused funding primarily on substance abuse treatment, a different grouping of three programs focused its funding for health issues, another set of three focused on mental health and substance abuse treatment, and another set of three focused on employment. Because of the range in primary services that these programs fund, the overlap in this area is minimal as well.

Table 4. Variations in Population Targets across Federal Reentry Grant Programs, Fiscal Year 2011

Department	**Grant program**	Reentry population is the exclusive target of the program and all solicitations	At least one grant solicitation targets the reentry population	Corrections or criminal justice is the target but funds can be used for reentry
Justice	Second Chance Act	X		
	Residential Substance Abuse Treatment for State Prisoners		X	
	Edward Byrne Memorial Justice Assistance Grant			X
	Justice and Mental Health Collaboration		X	
Labor	Reintegration of Ex-Offenders	X		
Health and Human Services	Programs of Regional and National Significance (includes the Offender Reentry Program)		X	
	Healthy Marriage Promotion and Responsible Fatherhood Grants		X	

Table 4. (Continued)

Department	**Grant program**	Reentry population is the exclusive target of the program and all solicitations	At least one grant solicitation targets the reentry population	Corrections or criminal justice is the target but funds can be used for reentry
	The Linkage to Life Program: Rebuilding Broken Bridges for Minority Families Impacted by HIV/AIDS		X	
	Health Improvement for Re-entering Ex-offenders Initiative	X		

Source: GAO analysis of grant solicitations.

When considering the three areas together—applicant eligibility, targeting of services, and primary services funded—the overall overlap is minimal. Specifically, there were variations in the applicant eligibility standards and target populations, even when grant programs allowed spending for the provision of similar services. For example, Labor's reentry program limits eligibility to private, nonprofit organizations that will use the funds primarily to assist current or former inmates—residing in or released from any facility—with their employment needs. In contrast, one of DOJ's reentry programs limits eligibility to governmental entities that will use the funds primarily to assist current or former inmates—residing in or released from state, local, or tribal facilities—with their substance abuse treatment needs. As we have previously reported, having multiple agencies with varying expertise involved in delivering services can be advantageous.[35] For example, agencies may be better able to tailor programs to suit their specific missions and needs. We have also previously reported that overlap among grant programs may be desirable because such overlap can enable granting agencies to leverage multiple funding streams to serve a single purpose.

Table 5. Variations in Primary Services Funded across Federal Reentry Grant Programs, Fiscal Year 2011

		Primary services funded							
Department	*Grant program*	*Employment (Includes education and vocational training)*	*Housing*	*Health*	*Mental or behavioral health*	*Substance abuse*	*Life, family, and parenting skills*	*Reentry courts*[a]	*None, general correctionsthat could be used forreentry*
Justice	Second Chance Act	X	X	X	X	X	X	X	
	Residential Substance Abuse Treatment for State Prisoners					X			
	Edward Byrne Memorial Justice Assistance Grant								X
	Justice and Mental Health Collaboration				X	X			
Labor	Reintegration of Ex-Offenders	X							
Health and Human Services	Programs of Regional and National Significance (includes the Offender Reentry Program)				X	X			
	Healthy Marriage Promotion and Responsible Fatherhood Grants	X					X		

Table 5. (Continued)

		Primary services funded							
Department	*Grant program*	*Employment (Includes education and vocational training)*	*Housing*	*Health*	*Mental or behavioral health*	*Substance abuse*	*Life, family, and parenting skills*	*Reentry courts*[a]	*None, general correctionsthat could be used forreentry*
	The Linkage to Life Program: Rebuilding Broken Bridges for Minority Families Impacted by HIV/AIDS			X					
	Health Improvement for Re-entering Ex-offenders Initiative			X					

Source: GAO analysis of grant solicitations.

[a] According to the SCA solicitation for reentry courts, a reentry court is designed to leverage partnerships among courts, social services, and the community to facilitate successful reentry. Reentry courts necessitate considerable cooperation between corrections and local judiciaries, since they require the active involvement of community corrections agencies or parole boards in transitioning former inmates back into the community through active judicial or executive branch oversight. On its solicitation, DOJ does not define a specific model for reentry courts.

For example, according to DOJ officials, they encourage grantees to use multiple streams of funding to fully implement their projects when local and federal funding is limited.

Further, federal agency officials from DOJ, Labor, and HHS stated that reentry can be enhanced by coinvestment—where a variety of entities in one community are receiving funds from multiple sources to assist with reentry—as these reentry programs can complement one another. We observed the benefits of this coinvestment when we interviewed grantees. For example, one of the nine grantees we interviewed received funds in 2011 from two different grant programs—ORP and RExO. These two funding streams helped the grantee provide both substance abuse treatment and employment assistance to the reentry population it served. Another grantee received a HHS Healthy Marriage Promotion and Responsible Fatherhood Grant in fiscal year 2011, and also received a RExO grant in 2012. The former assisted fathers reentering the community to develop parenting, relationship, and money management skills, while the latter grant would be used to assist both male and female former inmates with obtaining employment. Further, a few grantees stressed that the reentry population had various needs and that it is important that not just one need be met, but that the full array of services be available to prevent recidivism. According to Labor officials, given the volume of ex-offenders that are released each year, competition for limited reentry assistance from service providers in their communities is stiff. Of the more than 700,000 inmates released each year, according to each agency's most recent annual data, the SCA program provided services to approximately 6,600; the RExO program provided services to about 7,500; and the ORP program provided services to about 3,300.[36]

Although the overlap is minimal across applicant eligibility, program targeting, and the services the grant programs fund—and the risk for duplication is therefore low—we have previously reported that the existence of overlapping grant programs is an indication that agencies should increase their awareness of where their funds are going.[37] We have also reported that in addition to increasing their individual awareness, granting agencies should coordinate to ensure that any resulting duplication in grant award funding is purposeful rather than unnecessary. According to DOJ officials, it is in the best interest of each agency to know where there is active overlap between existing inmate reentry projects, as this allows for coordination of service delivery and the leveraging of federal resources, if appropriate. As we discuss in the next section of this report, DOJ, Labor, and HHS have implemented a number of mechanisms, partly in recognition of the overlap that does exist, to coordinate their granting efforts. Furthermore, officials acknowledge that even more can be done to increase awareness over the flow of federal funds and manage the risk, however low it may be, of unnecessary duplication.

AGENCIES HAVE TAKEN STEPS TO COORDINATE THEIR REENTRY PROGRAMS AND FURTHER REDUCE THE POTENTIAL FOR UNNECESSARY DUPLICATION IN FUNDING

Agencies Have Acknowledged Where Overlap Exists and Have Taken Steps to Coordinate Efforts

With acknowledgment of some overlap, DOJ, Labor, and HHS have taken a variety of steps to coordinate their reentry efforts as a means to prevent unnecessary duplication and share promising practices. The steps are consistent with best practices for interagency collaboration,[38] and include intra- and interagency working groups, the collective Federal Interagency Reentry Council, and a national resource center to obtain information, such as promising practices.

Intra-agency coordination. Recognizing some overlap across their grant programs, both DOJ and HHS developed intra-agency working groups to internally coordinate their reentry efforts. For example, DOJ launched Project Reentry in 2010 to "focus federal resources on increasing public safety and maximizing the efficient use of public safety dollars by reducing recidivism rates." According to DOJ officials, DOJ has some of the same members on Project Reentry as it has on the Federal Interagency Reentry Council to ensure that communication and collaboration is in place between the two groups. According to DOJ officials, Project Reentry provides opportunities for DOJ components to communicate; coordinate; brainstorm; and implement projects, initiatives, and ideas focused on improving outcomes in prisoner reentry. Efforts of Project Reentry include organizing workshops on reentry issues and supporting reentry courts by developing a tool kit on reentry. According to HHS officials, in 2010, its working group developed an agency-wide inventory of HHS efforts to assist incarcerated and reentering individuals and their families. According to a HHS official from the office that coordinated the inventory efforts, the primary purpose of the inventory is to serve as a resource document so that HHS officials are aware of what projects are going on and who is working on them. Although the official stated that the working group no longer has regular meetings, members now informally coordinate and participate in the Federal Interagency Reentry Council.

Interagency coordination. Agency officials from DOJ, Labor, and HHS report that they have developed strong partnerships with their counterpart grant makers as a result of prior collaborative initiatives, such as SVORI and PRI. Although officials from DOJ and HHS reported that some of this grant coordination is informal and ad hoc, DOJ, Labor, and HHS have developed more formal and ongoing coordination mechanisms, as well. For example, DOJ's Bureau of Justice Assistance and HHS's Substance Abuse and Mental Health Services Administration first developed a memorandum of understanding in 2009 to improve formal coordination and communication in various programmatic areas, including reentry. Specifically, the agreement states that these agencies will coordinate on the development of grant solicitations, grantee conferences, and the vetting of relevant publications, among other things. Reference to this agreement is also included in subsequent ORP grant solicitations, stating that these agencies "share a mutual interest in supporting and shaping offender reentry-treatment services, as both agencies fund 'offender reentry' programs ... ORP grantees will be expected to seek out and coordinate with any local federally-funded offender reentry initiatives including 'Second Chance Act' offender reentry programs, as appropriate." The memorandum assists these agencies in establishing a mutually reinforcing or joint strategy, consistent with best practices for interagency collaboration. Agency officials reported that their interagency coordination has encouraged personal relationships among grant-administering staff and as a result, they are in contact at various phases in the grant life cycle. For example, officials from all three agencies said they are sharing some draft grant solicitations with one another to obtain feedback before issuing them. DOJ and Labor officials stated that they share the solicitations when the subject matter is relevant and not on a routine basis with all federal agencies. DOJ officials also stated that they are sharing lists of funded grant recipients with Labor, and that they publicly announce grant award decisions.

Federal Interagency Reentry Council. To enhance coordination across the federal agencies involved in reentry activities, the council's working group has taken several actions since its inception in 2011. Consistent with best practices for interagency collaboration, the council has helped agencies to define and articulate a common outcome, establish mutually reinforcing or joint strategies, identify and address needs by leveraging resources, and agree on roles and responsibilities. Specifically, the Federal Interagency Reentry Council has

- Inventoried all major federal reentry programs, including grant programs that supported reentry services in fiscal years 2009 and 2010, and Federal Interagency Reentry Council officials stated that they continue to update the inventory to include resources available in 2011 and future years. According to HHS officials, the council modeled this effort after HHS's initiative to develop its intra-agency inventory. Further, HHS officials stated that understanding what resources are available is the first step to preventing unnecessary duplication.
- Convened research staff from 12 of its member agencies to regularly share information about reentry research and identify opportunities for research collaboration. Supporting the collaborative efforts of the council, officials from HHS, DOJ, and the Department of Commerce's Census Bureau convened a research conference in January 2012 to discuss developing and improving federal household survey measures relating to incarceration. According to a HHS official, such measures would increase knowledge of the effects of incarceration and reentry on individuals and their families.
- Working with the Office of Management and Budget, developed an interagency intranet site for the council, which allows all federal agencies to share key documents and resources. Information included on the site includes PowerPoint briefings and reentry-related recommendations.

In addition to its efforts to coordinate across federal reentry grant programs, according to member agency officials, the Federal Interagency Reentry Council has been focused on reducing the barriers that exist for the reentry population. For example, the council has taken several actions to address collateral consequences of criminal convictions—these are the laws and policies that restrict former inmates from things such as employment, welfare benefits, access to public housing, and eligibility for student loans for higher education. Such collateral penalties place substantial barriers to an individual's social and economic advancement and can challenge successful reentry. Appendix II provides a summary of the council's efforts to reduce reentry barriers and to achieve its other goals.

The National Reentry Resource Center. The Second Chance Act provided for the establishment of the National Reentry Resource Center, which was established in 2008.39 DOJ partially funds the center, and under a cooperative agreement, the Council of State Governments Justice Center manages it.40 The center's staff provide education, training, and technical assistance to states, tribes, territories, local governments, service providers, nonprofit organizations, and corrections institutions working on reentry issues. The National Reentry Resource Center's mission is to advance the reentry field through knowledge transfer and dissemination and to promote evidence-based best practices. Some of the activities the National Reentry Resource Center staff, along with key stakeholders, have undertaken include the development of the Reentry Services Directories, National Criminal Justice Initiatives Map, a library of reentry resources, and a website known as the What Works in Reentry Clearinghouse, among other things.

- *Reentry Service Directories.* In 2009, the National Reentry Resource Center catalogued state-led reentry efforts and launched a nationwide online directory of state reentry coordinators. Understanding the important role local governments play in reentry, in partnership with other stakeholders, the center has expanded the directories to include city- and county-led initiatives.
- *National Criminal Justice Initiatives Map.* Taking the inventory on federal reentry resources that the Federal Interagency Reentry Council assembled, the National Reentry Resource Center developed an online, interactive map that highlights major federal reentry initiatives and identifies reentry grantees in every state. The map seeks to provide a place-based catalog of national initiatives and programs designed to reduce the recidivism rates of people returning from prison, jail, and juvenile facilities. According to Federal Interagency Reentry Council and Council of State Governments Justice Center officials, this resource allows both federal staff and local stakeholders to identify reentry resources in their jurisdictions and coordinate more effectively at the local level. However, at present, the map does not include the flow of funds to subgrantees. For example, one grantee we interviewed in New York stated that its program did not provide direct services in the New York area—although the grantee is listed on the map as being a provider in New York. Rather, the grantee stated that its program provided funds to four of its affiliates in other states. Council of State Governments Justice Center officials stated that the

map is based on the Federal Interagency Reentry Council's inventory and is for informational purposes. Further, Federal Interagency Reentry Council officials stated that they continually work to update the inventory, and associated map, and that these efforts mark the first step to visually depicting the general flow of federal dollars. Five of the nine grantees we interviewed reported utilizing the map and finding it very useful. For example, three grantees reported that it was useful in helping them identify other resources in their jurisdictions. Three other grantees that had not used the map stated that they think it would be useful for future use.

- Library of reentry resources. The web-based library includes documents of interest to state and local policymakers, community and faith-based organizations, and the reentry population. Resources are organized by topic, such as juveniles, sex offenders, substance abuse, and mental health and include publications authored by organizations, researchers, service providers, and practitioners working in the reentry field.
- What Works in Reentry Clearinghouse. This website—launched in 2012—offers access to research on the effectiveness of a wide variety of reentry programs and practices. According to the website, it provides a one-stop shop for practitioners and service providers seeking guidance on evidence-based reentry interventions, as well as a useful resource for researchers and others interested in reentry. The clearinghouse currently includes information on employment, housing, and mental health, and the National Reentry Resource Center has plans to add additional issue areas. Since the site was recently launched, it is too soon to assess how grantees are using this website to inform their program design and implementation.

Other efforts to share promising practices across agencies. In addition to some of the efforts listed above, DOJ, Labor, and HHS have, for example, held conferences or meetings for their grantees so that they may meet with one another, learn from panelists and presenters, and share information. DOJ officials stated that for the first time, in May 2012, its SCA conference was open to other federal agency reentry grantees. The grantees we interviewed stated that this type of coordination with other grantees has been, or would be, very useful, and that they learn information about other grantees through mechanisms such as conference calls and through their technical advisers. In addition, all three agencies share information on their agency websites about promising practices to sustain successful reentry efforts. Specifically, DOJ maintains the Crime Solutions website—CrimeSolutions.gov—which includes information to assist users with practical decision making and program implementation on specific justice-related programs, including reentry, and presents the existing evaluation research against standard criteria. The CrimeSolutions.gov and What Works in Reentry Clearinghouse are linked to each other. Further, Labor maintains a website for its RExO grantees to share information, such as stories of efforts of grantees, and HHS officials stated that they are in the process of fully implementing a similar website. Finally, the Council of State Governments Justice Center, with support from DOJ, launched a reentry program database in 2010, which highlights community-based reentry programs that self-report promising practices and policies that facilitate successful reentry.

Agencies Have Taken Action, or Have Actions Under Way, to Further Reduce the Risk of Unnecessary Duplication

In addition to the steps that DOJ, Labor, and HHS have taken—independently and through the Federal Interagency Reentry Council—to coordinate reentry efforts, they have also taken, or plan to take, further action to reduce the potential that grantees are using funds from different agencies or programs for the same purpose. As our prior work at DOJ has shown, if an applicant, either as a grantee or as a subgrantee, receives multiple grant awards from overlapping programs, the risk of unnecessary duplication increases, since the applicant may receive funding from more than one source for the same purpose without federal agencies being aware that this situation exists. Such duplication may be unnecessary if, for example, the total funding received exceeds the applicant's need, or if neither granting agency was aware of the original funding decision.[41] To help guard against this, HHS requires its reentry grantees to provide current or potential funding information from applicants. Officials stated that they have used this information for some grant programs to help ensure that funds will not be awarded for activities that are already supported by other agencies. Further, in response to our findings and recommendations from prior work, which specifically addressed issues of overlap and the importance of DOJ having awareness of the other sources of funds that applicants may have applied for or are receiving, DOJ has plans under way to assess all of its grant programs to determine the extent of any unnecessary duplication.[42]

Further, DOJ plans to use the results of this assessment to determine how it will require grant applicants to report on other federal funding for the same purposes that they currently receive or have recently applied for in their grant applications.[43] DOJ is also currently piloting such a requirement for a limited number of programs. Although Labor currently makes funding decisions without asking for information about and regularly considering other sources of an applicant's federal funding to carry out the same or similar activities, it also has plans under way to collect and incorporate this information into its future grant solicitations. Labor officials acknowledged the benefits of collecting this information in helping to further prevent duplication, and toward the end of our audit work, told us that they have held meeting with HHS officials to learn how HHS collects this information from its grantees. As of early November, 2012, Labor officials revised one of the department's RExO grant solicitations to include a requirement that prospective grantees report other federal funding sources in their applications. Revisions to this solicitation were in final review, and officials stated that once it is approved, they plan to include this requirement in all future RExO grant applications

AGENCIES ARE MEASURING GRANTEE PERFORMANCE AND CONDUCTING PROGRAM EVALUATIONS, BUT ADDITIONAL INFORMATION SHARING COULD BE BENEFICIAL

Agencies Require Grantees to Collect Information on a Variety of Metrics to Assess Grantees' Performance

To assess individual grantee performance, DOJ, Labor, and HHS require their SCA, RExO, and ORP grantees to collect information on a variety of metrics, including those specific to recidivism.[44] According to DOJ's Bureau of Justice Statistics, there is no single definition of recidivism that is used universally.[45] Instead, recidivism is composed of multiple measures, including, rearrest, reconviction, or a return to jail or prison with or without a new sentence—all of which indicate an individual's return to the criminal justice system.[46] Therefore, agencies require grantees to collect information on measures such as the number of program participants who are arrested or reincarcerated. In some cases, federal agencies may include all these measures in their assessment of how well grantees are doing to help inmates successfully transition to nonprison life. In other cases, an agency may use fewer measures.

For the SCA grant program, DOJ defines recidivism as "a return to prison and/or jail with either a new conviction or as a result of a violation of the terms of supervision within 12 months of initial release." Although DOJ officials have established a goal that SCA programs should reduce recidivism, they have not set a specific numeric target. Instead, officials stated that they compare the results individual grantees report in reducing recidivism with the average across all SCA grantees. DOJ officials stated that they are waiting for the results of an ongoing SCA program evaluation, which we discuss later in this report, so that they will have more information to determine what, if any, numerical targets would be most appropriate and what effect the SCA program has had on recidivism. Although DOJ officials have been collecting recidivism data from SCA grantees quarterly, they stated that they cannot use these data to determine the program's impact on recidivism because they have concerns with the validity and reliability of data. Specifically, according to DOJ officials, some SCA grantees experienced difficulties accessing recidivism data, and as a result, data may not accurately reflect the criminal justice outcomes of the participants after they receive reentry services. For example, a grantee that is a county jail facility may not have access to criminal justice data outside its jurisdiction, which makes it difficult to track if a participant commits another crime in a different jurisdiction.

To help address data reliability challenges, DOJ officials stated that, as of October 2012, they will require SCA grantees to report on recidivism measures once at the end of their grant period rather than every quarter, as previously required. DOJ officials told us that they believe the reduced frequency in reporting will give grantees more time to access and review data they acquire from secondary sources and result in numbers that more accurately reflect recidivism outcomes. In addition, DOJ officials stated that this change will provide DOJ staff with more time to provide SCA grantees targeted technical assistance in data collection and reporting, which they believe will help mitigate the challenge of acquiring data from secondary sources. In another step to help ensure the reliability of data DOJ collects, the department requires SCA grantees to report on the source of their data, as well as any steps taken to ensure its validity.

For the RExO grant program, Labor defines recidivism as those cases in which an individual is "re-arrested for a new crime or re-incarcerated for revocation of the parole or probation order within 1 year of their release from prison." If a participant is rearrested and subsequently released without being convicted of a new crime during that time, Labor stipulates that RExO grantees may remove these participants from the recidivism rate. Using this definition, Labor has set a target goal for its grantees that no more than 22 percent of all the participants a grantee serves should recidivate, which is half the national rate of recidivism at 12 months.[47] Labor reported to Congress as part of its fiscal year 2013 Congressional Budget Justification that RExO grantees have achieved this goal with an average of 14 percent of RExO participant's recidivating. However, Labor officials stated that recidivism can be a difficult outcome measure to track and they have had some concerns about the accuracy of data reported by grantees. As a result, according to Labor officials, they require RExO grantees to maintain documentation supporting the recidivism outcomes they report. During RExO program operations site visits, Labor officials stated that they review case files to ensure grantees are maintaining this documentation. Further, on an annual basis, Labor officials stated that they review all the performance data RExO grantees submit to ensure program outcomes have been reported for all participants. Additionally, Labor officials stated that the ongoing RExO program evaluation, discussed later in this report, will independently verify the recidivism outcomes reported by grantees.

Although HHS officials stated that the department does not collect data on recidivism from its ORP grantees because no single definition of recidivism is used universally, HHS does require ORP grantees to report on the "criminal justice status" of program participants, which includes information on their arrest or incarceration. Using its definition, HHS has set a target goal for its grantees that 95 percent of all participants will have reported having no involvement with the criminal justice system for the 30 days prior to the reporting period—or no more than 5 percent of all participants reporting involvement with the criminal justice system during this time. HHS reported to Congress in its fiscal year 2013 Congressional Budget Justification that its ORP grantees active in fiscal year 2011 achieved this goal with 4.8 percent of participants' reporting involvement with the criminal justice system during the 30 days prior to the reporting period. In contrast to Labor's requirement that RExO grantees maintain documentation supporting the recidivism outcomes they report, HHS requires ORP grantees to have their participants self-report any interaction with the criminal justice system for the 30 days prior to each reporting period. According to HHS officials, they take steps to validate data and perform periodic audits to ensure their validity. Table 6 provides an overview of the measures each agency collects from its grantees to indicate recidivism.

Table 6. Federal Agencies' Recidivism-Related Measures

Department	Grant program	Recidivism-related measures
Justice	Second Chance Act	Number of participants who were arrested for a new offense Number of participants who were convicted of a new offense Number of participants who had a revocation of the terms of supervised release Number of participants who were reincarcerated[a]
Labor	Reintegration Of Ex-Offenders	Number of participants who were rearrested for a new crime Number of participant reincarcerated for revocation of a parole or probation order
Health and Human Services	Offender Reentry Program[b]	Number of arrests Number of arrests for drug-related offenses Number of nights spent in jail or prison

Source: GAO analysis of DOJ, Labor, and HHS data.

[a] Prior to fiscal year 2012, DOJ also required SCA grantees to report on the number of participants who had a technical violation of supervised release. DOJ officials stated that this measure was removed as of October 2012 because it was the most problematic for SCA grantees to report on consistently and the least likely to indicate criminal behavior.

[b] The Offender Reentry Program is a grant solicitation under HHS's Programs of Regional and National Significance.

In addition to recidivism-specific metrics, DOJ, Labor, and HHS also require grantees to collect and report on performance information related to other grant purposes. For example, Labor's RExO program is focused on reducing recidivism through employment assistance. Accordingly, Labor officials also require its grantees to monitor and report on the percentage of participants who enter employment, the employment retention rate, and the average earnings of program participants. Similarly, as HHS's ORP program aims to expand or enhance substance abuse treatment and related recovery, HHS officials require its grantees to monitor and report on the rate of substance abuse relapse and the number of participants who receive inpatient or outpatient treatment. Further, DOJ developed a core set of performance measures that all SCA grantees are required to report on, such as the rate of successful program completion, but it also includes metrics particular to the specific SCA solicitation. For instance, since the SCA Family-Based Prisoner Substance Abuse Treatment solicitation requires grantees to involve families in treatment services, DOJ requires grantees to report on the number of family members who participate in services.

Agencies Analyze Grantee Performance Data to Improve Operations but Additional Information Sharing Could Be Beneficial

DOJ, Labor, and HHS analyze recidivism data to improve grant program operations in a variety of ways, but agencies could enhance information sharing about the methods they use to collect and analyze data to determine and report on overall program effectiveness.

Agencies require their reentry program grantees to submit performance reports, at varying intervals, using their respective web-based grant management systems. According to officials from all three agencies, they use data grantees provide to determine the effectiveness of individual grantees. If data indicate a problem, officials stated that they may visit a grantee's operations in person or otherwise provide targeted technical assistance to improve program outcomes. Table 7 describes the systems each agency uses, the frequency with which grantees are required to report, and the frequency with which agencies analyze grantee data.

The grant management systems DOJ, Labor, and HHS use to monitor grantee effectiveness have different functionalities that present different benefits to agencies and grantees in collecting and analyzing performance data to improve operations. Specifically, Labor and HHS require RExO and ORP grantees to use MIS and SAIS to submit performance reports. Although grantees are required to submit reports to Labor and HHS on a quarterly or semiannual basis, because the systems allow grantees to enter participant-level data directly, grantees may enter these data more frequently for case management purposes.

In fact, both agencies expect their grantees to use the systems as case management tools. According to HHS officials, they require ORP grantees to regularly enter participant-level data and provide data analysis training so grantees can use data to inform program decisions. For instance, HHS officials stated that ORP grantees use SAIS to aggregate data to identify trends or gaps in services and then make adjustments as needed in their operations. Further, two RExO grantees we met with reported finding Labor's MIS system useful, as they could use a single system for both case management and grant-reporting purposes.

Table 7. Agencies' Use of Grant Management Systems for Performance Reporting and Analysis

Department	Grant management systems	Frequency grantees submit reports	Frequency agencies analyze data
Justice	Performance Measurement Tool (PMT) collects quantitative grantee performance information, such as data on recidivism outcomes and participant enrollment among others.	Quarterly, except recidivism data, which are required once during the grant period	Quarterly, except recidivism outcomes, which are considered once at the end of the grant period
	Grants Management System (GMS) collects narrative performance information, such as program successes and challenges over the reporting period[a]	Semiannually	Semiannually
Labor	Management Information System (MIS) collects quantitative information such as data on recidivism outcomes and employment rates.	Quarterly, although grantees can use MIS for case management and enter data more frequently	Weekly and quarterly
Health and Human Services	Service Accountability Improvement System (SAIS) collects quantitative information such as data on recidivism outcomes and substance abuse relapse.	Semiannually, although grantees can use SAIS for case management and enter data more frequently	Bimonthly and semiannually

Source: GAO analysis of DOJ, Labor and HHS data.

[a] For the semiannual reports, DOJ requires SCA grantees to provide narrative responses to seven questions: (1) What were your accomplishments within this reporting period? (2) What goals were accomplished, as they relate to your grant application? (3) What problems/barriers did you encounter, if any, within the reporting period that prevented you from reaching your goals or milestones? (4) Is there any assistance that [DOJ] can provide to address any problems/barriers identified in question #3? (5) Are you on track to fiscally and programmatically complete your program as outlined in your grant application? (6) What major activities are planned for the next 6 months? (7) Based on your knowledge of the criminal justice field, are there any innovative programs/accomplishments that you would like to share with BJA?

In contrast, one SCA grantee we interviewed stated that it had to develop its own case management systems to track participant-level data, since DOJ requires its grantees to enter aggregate, rather than participant-level, data into DOJ's PMT.

Because RExO and ORP grantees can use MIS and SAIS to enter participant-level data and may do so on a more frequent basis, Labor and HHS officials can monitor and take action in response to those data. For instance, Labor officials use MIS to generate a weekly report that provides them with a snapshot of performance across all RExO grantees. According to officials, they can review data from the weekly report to see how many participants entered employment or who was arrested or reincarcerated. If data reveal that a particular grantee is showing a lower than expected rate of entered employment or other result indicating a program challenge, Labor officials stated that they take action to work with the grantee to identify resources and technical assistance that could improve the performance outcome. One RExO grantee we met with stated that Labor technical assistants visited its operations site about three or four times each year for the duration of its grant and provided helpful assistance that the grantee believes resulted in increased program participation. Similarly, according to HHS officials, they use SAIS on an ongoing basis to monitor performance across ORP grantees. According to program officials, if SAIS data indicate an issue, they can initiate on-site clinical or administrative technical assistance on an as-needed basis to improve a program outcome. In contrast, DOJ collects aggregate-level data through PMT, which DOJ officials stated that they review quarterly. In addition, for certain grant programs, DOJ employs a semiannual review process that it calls GrantStat. Officials stated that during a GrantStat review, they assess PMT performance data and other relevant information, such as grantees' semiannual narrative reports and input from DOJ's technical assistance providers. DOJ's goal during GrantStat is to determine how effective an overall grant program is in meeting its goals and which grantees may need targeted technical assistance, and in which areas, to improve their operations and participant outcomes. While DOJ has applied the GrantStat review process to several programs that it funds—as resources have permitted—officials stated that they used GrantStat specifically to assess the performance of selected SCA grantees in April and May 2011. As a result, DOJ officials stated that they had a better understanding of the quality of data that SCA grantees submit using PMT. They also stated that the assessment helped inform future funding decisions, such as which SCA grants funded in fiscal year 2009 should be continued.

According to DOJ officials, planning is under way to determine the programs that will be prioritized next for GrantStat review.

Although agency officials stated that they have had discussions about the capabilities of their systems, agencies have not formally met with one another, or through the Federal Interagency Reentry Council, to discuss the relative strengths and challenges of their systems, how frequently they collect and analyze grantee performance data, and how they determine overall program effectiveness. For example, according to Labor officials, they provided an informational overview of MIS to HHS officials, and provided HHS with access to MIS so officials could test the functionality of the system. In addition, DOJ officials stated that they had informational discussions with other members of the Federal Interagency Reentry Council, particularly Labor, about their performance measurement systems. Part of the Federal Interagency Reentry Council's mission is to enhance communication, coordination, and collaboration across federal agency reentry initiatives. Further, we have previously reported on the importance of interagency coordination and information sharing across federal entities.[48] We have also reported on the importance of measuring performance.[49] By maximizing existing information-sharing and collaborative forums, such as the one the Federal Interagency Reentry Council affords, all three agencies would have an opportunity to share information on (1) what data they collect, (2) how often they review and analyze data, and (3) what decisions their analyses inform to improve program operations and report results, as well as to consider the feasibility of adopting any promising practices as appropriate. DOJ, Labor, and HHS generally agreed that information sharing of this kind would be useful. Discussions going forward would need to consider things such as the design of each system, the strengths and limitations of the respective grant management systems vis-à-vis each agency's grant management policies and requirements, and the cost and benefits of adopting promising practices.

DOJ and Labor Have Commissioned Program Evaluations, and Efforts Are Ongoing to Determine Program Effectiveness in Reducing Recidivism

In addition to the program-monitoring activities that agencies have taken at the individual grantee level, DOJ and Labor have spent approximately $22 million to commission program evaluations to assess the effectiveness of selected reentry grant programs. Program evaluations are individual systematic studies conducted periodically or on an ad hoc basis to assess how well a program is working. They are often conducted by experts external to the program, inside or outside the agency, as well as by program managers. As we have previously reported, for programs where outcomes, such as reducing recidivism, may not be achieved quickly, or where their relationship to the program is uncertain, program evaluations may be needed in addition to performance measurement, to examine the extent to which a program is achieving its objectives.[50] Accordingly, DOJ and Labor have commissioned program evaluations, examples of which are listed below.

- The Second Chance Act authorizes DOJ's National Institute of Justice to evaluate the effectiveness of the SCA projects funded using a methodology that generates evidence of which reentry approaches and strategies are most effective.[51] Accordingly, the National Institute of Justice commissioned evaluations of grant programs funded under two SCA solicitations—SCA Reentry Courts and SCA Adult Demonstration. DOJ estimates that a report providing final results for the SCA Reentry Courts will be completed in summer 2015 and that a report providing interim results of the SCA Adult Demonstration program will be completed in spring 2013. DOJ officials also told us that a report with final results of the SCA Adult Demonstration program should be completed in summer 2015.
- Labor commissioned a program evaluation of its RExO grant program with officials expecting final results in June 2014. The evaluation began in fiscal year 2008 and examines impacts on participants' post-program labor market outcomes and rates of recidivism by comparing outcomes of RExO participants with the outcomes of randomly assigned individuals who are eligible for but do not receive RExO services.

See appendix III for summary information regarding ongoing DOJ and Labor ongoing program evaluations.

The findings of these evaluations will likely add to the information agencies have to demonstrate the overall effectiveness of these programs as currently implemented in reducing recidivism. But because these evaluations are ongoing, it limits the available evidence agencies' have to demonstrate their effectiveness in reducing recidivism. Nevertheless, agencies already have the results of program evaluations that Labor and DOJ commissioned for PRI and SVORI—predecessor reentry programs to SCA and RExO that were intended to reduce recidivism. In terms of recidivism, the final PRI program evaluation published in January 2009 concluded that recidivism rates across all grantees appeared low at 1 year postrelease.[52] However, the report noted that findings on recidivism should be interpreted with caution because "while [Labor] required grantees to verify and document that participants were not re-arrested before entering data into MIS, site visits revealed that some grantee staff used a 'no news is good news' approach by recording that participants had not recidivated, even if they were not able to verify the outcome." The report stated that recidivism outcome data were missing for about 12 percent of PRI program participants. Additionally, as noted in the evaluation report, the study did not include a control or comparison group and therefore was not intended to assess the effectiveness of PRI at improving program outcomes. DOJ's National Institute of Justice's evaluation of the SVORI program concluded that when compared with nonprogram participants, SVORI participants showed no discernible differences on outcomes with respect to recidivism.[53] A subsequent report funded by DOJ concluded in February 2012 that additional research was necessary into the sequencing and effects of specific combinations of reentry services and that a longer follow-up period with program participants may be necessary to observe the positive effects of the SVORI program on participants' criminal behavior and interactions with the criminal justice system.[54] According to DOJ officials, the design of the ongoing SCA Adult Demonstration evaluation includes assessing the types, intensity, and quality of the services being provided over 3 years.

Further, a 2010 DOJ Inspector General report identified program deficiencies with both PRI and SVORI.[55] For instance, the report found that SVORI and PRI grantees were not required to identify a baseline recidivism rate that would be needed to calculate any changes in recidivism rates as a result of the program. Additionally, SVORI solicitations issued between 2002 and 2004 did not specify a time frame after release in which to track a program participant's recidivism. As noted in the Inspector General report, a time frame after release in which to track recidivism outcomes is needed so that progress can be demonstrated and outcomes compared at varying points during the monitoring period. In addition, the report recommended, among other things, that agencies require reentry grantees to establish baseline recidivism rates to facilitate comparison of recidivism rates between participants of reentry programs and nonparticipants. For both the SCA and RExO reentry grant programs, DOJ and Labor have taken steps to address some of the deficiencies. For example, DOJ requires its SCA grantees to provide a baseline recidivism rate they can use later to determine program impact, if any, on recidivism. Additionally, both DOJ and Labor have specified a 12-month time frame after release from prison or jail by which to measure recidivism. Further, according to Labor officials, as a result of the deficiencies identified with the PRI and SVORI programs, the department implemented several steps, including annually reviewing data, to ensure the reliability and validity of the recidivism data that RExO grantees report.

In contrast, HHS officials stated that although they do conduct program evaluations, they have not done this for ORP because of its size compared with other HHS grant programs. According to HHS's Office of the Inspector General, HHS is the largest grant-making organization in the federal government, awarding $370 billion in grants in fiscal year 2010.[56] However, HHS does permit ORP grantees to spend up to 20 percent of their grant funds on program evaluations and data collection. According to HHS officials, they collect and periodically review these evaluations and have used the findings, alongside other research, to change elements of program design. For example, officials stated that they changed the ORP solicitation to require that grantees work with correctional facilities to ensure a smoother transition and greater continuity of treatment services as an inmate transitions to community-based treatment. However, officials stated that the majority of performance data they use to analyze ORP's overall program effectiveness is gathered through the information individual grantees report using SAIS.

CONCLUSION

Given the number of federal agencies involved in reentry, the high levels of recidivism, and current resource constraints facing the federal government, it is important that federal agencies be well aware of how their grant funds are spent and monitor grantee performance to ensure the highest return on federal investment. Accordingly, federal agencies have taken a variety of actions to enhance coordination to prevent unnecessary duplication and monitor grantees performance. These actions include developing a memorandum of understanding to improve formal coordination and communication, sharing draft grant solicitations with one another to obtain feedback before issuing them, and inventorying all major federal reentry programs. Additionally, as multiple agencies are involved in federal efforts to reduce recidivism, they have an opportunity to learn from one another about promising approaches for collecting and analyzing data and making determinations about individual grantee and overall grant program effectiveness. Given that the effect of prior reentry efforts—SVORI and PRI—on recidivism was inconclusive, effective analysis of recidivism data gathered from current reentry programs is particularly important. However, DOJ, Labor, and HHS officials have not formally shared information on the relative strengths and limitations of the respective grant management systems and their unique approaches to monitoring outcomes. By taking action to share information on how well their grantees reduce recidivism, agencies could leverage existing collaborations, such as the Federal Interagency Reentry Council, and further strengthen their program management.

RECOMMENDATIONS FOR EXECUTIVE ACTION

To better utilize the performance information they collect from grantees, enhance the capacity of their respective grant management systems, and improve overall management of reentry programs designed to reduce recidivism, we recommend that the Attorney General, the Secretary of Labor, and the Secretary of Health and Human Services maximize existing information-sharing forums, such as the Federal Interagency Reentry Council, to (1) share details on how agencies collect and analyze their data, as well as how they determine program effectiveness, and (2) consider the feasibility of adapting any promising practices in the future.

AGENCY COMMENTS

We provided a draft of this report to DOJ, Labor, and HHS for comment. We received written comments from each. In addition, DOJ and HHS provided technical clarifications, which we incorporated where appropriate.

DOJ concurred with the recommendation in this report. Labor and HHS did not specifically state whether they concurred with our recommendation. All three departments reported that they would establish a subcommittee of the Federal Interagency Reentry Council Staff Working Group in the first quarter of fiscal year 2013 to (1) share performance measures, (2) assess and monitor grant performance information collected from grantees with a goal of improving overall management of reentry programs designed to reduce recidivism, and (3) communicate best practices for improving the coordinated delivery of evidenced-based services. These proposed steps, if implemented, would address the intent of our recommendation.

David C. Maurer,
Director
Homeland Security and Justice Issues

APPENDIX I: THE ROLE OF THE FEDERAL BUREAU OF PRISONS IN REENTRY

According to the Department of Justice's (DOJ) Federal Bureau of Prisons (BOP), the process of reentry begins the day an inmate is incarcerated, and generally should continue after an inmate is released. BOP considers reentry to be a high priority and includes it in its mission: "The mission of the BOP is to protect society by confining offenders in the controlled environments of prisons and community-based facilities that are safe, humane, cost-efficient, and appropriately secure, and to provide inmates with a range of work and other self-improvement programs that will help them adopt a crime-free lifestyle upon their return to the community."

BOP estimated that about $640 million of its $6.6 billion fiscal year 2012 operating budget is dedicated to reentry activities. According to BOP officials, the estimate is based on the costs of larger programs that specifically support reentry, such as education and vocational training initiatives and drug treatment programs. But officials stated that because reentry is a process and not a specific program, some initiatives that support reentry would not be captured in this estimate. For example, at a minimum, all BOP institutions offer the General Equivalency Diploma or English as a Second Language programs and therefore BOP included the costs of these programs as part of its reentry activities budget. However, the estimate does not include BOP-sponsored activities that are relevant to reentry that may be held on more of an ad hoc basis at individual BOP institutions. As we reported in September 2012, according to BOP officials, growth in the inmate population has led to increased waiting lists for programs.[1] For instance, as of the end of fiscal year 2011, about 2,400 inmates in male medium security institutions participated in residential drug treatment, almost 3,000 more inmates were on the waiting list to participate, and the average wait for enrollment exceeded 3 months. Table 8 illustrates the variety of reentry-related programs BOP provides.

Table 8. Selected BOP Inmate Reentry Programs and Activities

Reentry program categories	Examples of BOP reentry programs/activitiesa	Number of correctional facilities offering the program, fiscal year 2011	Program participants, fiscal year 2011
Drug treatment	Programs include the following: • Residential Drug Abuse Treatment Program: 9- to 12-month intensive drug abuse treatment program. • Non-Residential Drug Abuse Treatment Program: flexible program geared toward inmates with low-level substance abuse treatment needs. • Drug Abuse Education: program for inmates with a history of drug abuse that encourages self-examination on drug abuse and the cycle of crime. • Community Transition Drug Abuse Treatment: program supports the continuation of drug abuse treatment for inmates through their period of community transition.	Residential: 63 Non-Residential : all Drug Abuse Education: all Community Drug Transition is provided at Residential Reentry Centers.	Residential: 18,757 Non-Residential: 15,211 Drug Abuse Education: 41,243 Community Transition: 16,973
Education/ vocational training	Programs include General Equivalency Diploma, English as a Second Language, and Adult Continuing Education (includes classes such as computer literacy and financial planning, among others).	All correctional facilities offer General Equivalency Diploma, English as a Second Language, and Adult Continuing Education. Certain facilities may offer additional classes or workshops to supplement the primary curriculum.	General Equivalency Diploma: 20,979 English as a Second Language: 2,862 Continuing Education: 17,946

Table 8. (Continued)

Reentry program categories	Examples of BOP reentry programs/activitiesa	Number of correctional facilities offering the program, fiscal year 2011	Program participants, fiscal year 2011
Psychology services and sex offender management	Programs include the following: • Non-Residential Sex Offender Management: moderate intensity program primarily for first-time sexual offenders. • Residential Sex Offender Management: intensive program designed for sexual offenders convicted of multiple offenses. • Challenge: residential treatment program for high-security inmates with a history of substance abuse or mental illness. • Resolve: treatment program for female inmates with trauma-related mental illness.	Non-Residential Sex Offender Management: 5 Residential Sex Offender Management: 1 Challenge: 14 Resolve: 10	Non-Residential: 455 Residential: 112 Challenge: 1,979 Resolve: 2,198
Residential Reentry Centers	BOP contracts with Residential Reentry Centers to help facilitate an inmate's community transition. Centers provide inmates with employment counseling and job placement assistance, financial management assistance, and substance abuse treatment or counseling as well as other services, which may vary by facility.	All Residential Reentry Centers	72,494
Faith-based programs	Programs include Life Connections and Threshold. • Life Connections: 18-month multifaith-based residential program that includes mentoring and community service, among other things. • Threshold: 6- to 9-month nonresidential version of Life	Life Connections: 5 Threshold: 78	Life Connections: 394 Threshold: 757

Reentry program categories	Examples of BOP reentry programs/activitiesa	Number of correctional facilities offering the program, fiscal year 2011	Program participants, fiscal year 2011
	Connections.		
Release preparation program	Program includes classes or presentations providing employment assistance such as résumé preparation and job search strategies.	117	62,236

Source: GAO analysis of BOP documents.

[a] For residential programs, inmates live in a unit separate from the general BOP population. For nonresidential programs, inmates are typically housed among the general population.

Further, BOP developed a plan in 2011 to implement the Inmate Skills Development Initiative. Through this initiative, BOP intends to measure skills inmates acquired through effective programs with the goal of reducing rates of recidivism.

Once fully implemented, the process will involve identifying inmate strengths and weaknesses using a standardized assessment tool, linking programs used to identify specific deficit areas, and tracking the inmates' progress on their individualized plans throughout incarceration. According to BOP officials, correctional facilities are currently utilizing an assessment tool to measure inmates' skills, and consider the initiative's plan to be a living document that they will continue to update and improve.

In 2010, we reported on BOP's progress in implementing the Inmate Skills Development Initiative.[2]

In that report, we recommended that BOP develop a plan for implementing the initiative that includes key tasks, responsibilities and timelines, as well as a comprehensive cost estimate. BOP has since taken actions to implement these recommendations.

APPENDIX II: FEDERAL INTERAGENCY REENTRY COUNCIL ACCOMPLISHMENTS

The Attorney General convened the Federal Interagency Reentry Council for its first meeting on January 5, 2011. At that meeting, the council adopted a mission statement to (1) make communities safer by reducing recidivism and victimization, (2) assist those returning from prison and jail in becoming productive citizens, and (3) save taxpayer dollars by lowering the direct and collateral costs of incarceration. In addition, the council developed the following goals:

- identify research and evidence-based practices, policies, and programs that advance the council's mission around prisoner reentry and community safety;
- identify federal policy opportunities and barriers to improve outcomes for the reentry population;
- promote federal statutory, policy, and practice changes that focus on reducing crime and improving the well-being of formerly incarcerated individuals, their families, and communities;

- identify and support initiatives in the areas of education, employment, health, housing, faith, drug treatment, and family and community wellbeing that can contribute to successful outcomes for formerly incarcerated individuals;
- leverage resources across agencies that support this population in becoming productive citizens, and reducing recidivism and victimization; and
- coordinate messaging and communications about prisoner reentry and the administration's response to it.

According to the council, reentry is not only a public safety issue, but it also involves a variety of other issues, as shown in figure 2.

Source: Federal Interagency Reentry Coucil.

Figure 2. Issues Related to Reentry.

To address this wide range of issues, at its first meeting, the council developed a number of short-term issues on which to focus. These included

- providing visibility and transparency to federal reentry programs and policies,
- coordinating and leveraging federal resources for reentry, and
- removing federal barriers to reentry.

Council working group members, who currently represent 20 federal agencies, reported in 2011 and 2012 accomplishing several activities to achieve these short-term goals, some of which are highlighted in table 9.[1]

Table 9. Federal Interagency Reentry Council Accomplishments

Short-term goals	Accomplishments
Providing visibility and transparency to federal reentry programs and policies	• Reentry public education materials. Council agencies developed and disseminated a set of public education materials, including the Reentry Council Overview, and the Reentry MythBusters series. Reentry MythBusters are fact sheets designed to clarify existing federal policies that affect formerly incarcerated individuals and their families in areas such as public housing, access to benefits, parental rights, employer incentives, and more. • Website. Council agencies launched a website, which is housed within the Department of Justice-funded National Reentry Resource Center. The website provides public access to materials, activities, agency contacts, an interactive map of federal reentry resources, and a broad set of informational resources including the What Works in Reentry Clearinghouse. • Leadership and visibility. Leaders and staff from many of the council agencies highlighted reentry in speeches, meetings, congressional briefings, and testimonies in Washington, D.C. and around the country. They also held reentry-focused events and met with key stakeholder organizations, including the major state, city, and county associations; faith-based groups; research and policy organizations; foundations; advocates; and others. Council agencies have also contributed to recent statewide Reentry Summits.
Coordinating and leveraging federal resources for reentry	• Federal reentry inventory. Council agencies inventoried the major federal reentry resources going to states and localities. The National Reentry Resource Center then developed an interactive map that describes the major federal reentry initiatives and identifies active reentry grants in every state and by each federal agency. • Intranet site. The Office of Management and

Short-term goals	Accomplishments
	• Budget developed an interagency intranet site for the council, which allows all agencies to share material in one placc. • Collaborative reentry solicitations. Several agencies have collaborated to (1) develop new solicitations that reflect the reentry priorities of their agencies and/or (2) solicit input into and enhancc joint planning for their existing funding streams. • Reentry Researcher Network. Council agencies convened research staff from 12 federal agencies to share information about reentry research and identify opportunities for collaboration. The reentry researcher network is developing an inventory of reentry research under way and is hosting a series of research briefings on agency-funded projects. • National Reentry Conference. The Department of Justice-funded conference expanded its 2012 national conference of Second Chance grantees to include grantees from other federal agencies. • Women and reentry. The Department of Health and Human Services convened a conference focused exclusively on the reentry needs of women. • Reentry Policy Guidance and Toolkit for U.S. Attorneys. The Department of Justice issued new guidance about U.S. Attorney involvement in reentry efforts. The Department of Justice also developed a Reentry Toolkit for U.S. Attorneys, who are increasingly engaging in reentry efforts as part of their antiviolence strategies. • Federal Inter-branch Reentry Focus. The Department of Justice convened the U.S. Sentencing Commission, Administrative Office of the U.S. Courts, the Federal Judicial Center, and Bureau of Prisons to share information and consider coordinated reentry strategies for the federal criminal justice population.
Removing federal barriers to reentry	• *Reducing housing barriers and homelessness.* • The Housing and Urban Development Secretary and Assistant Secretary sent a letter to executive directors of public housing authorities explaining current federal regulations and informing local

Table 9. (Continued)

Short-term goals	Accomplishments
	public housing authorities that in many circumstances, formerly incarcerated people who have served their time should not be denied that access. Stating that "people who have paid their debt to society deserve the opportunity to become productive citizens and caring parents, to set the past aside and embrace the future. Part of that support means helping former inmates gain access to one of the most fundamental building blocks of a stable life—a place to live." • The United States Interagency Council on Homelessness published Searching Out Solutions: Constructive Alternatives to Criminalization, which focuses, in part, on effective housing strategies for the reentry population. • *Collateral consequences.* • The Attorney General wrote to state attorneys general asking them to review the collateral consequences of criminal convictions in their states and consider eliminating those that prevent reentering individuals from becoming productive members of their communities. • The Department of Justice is leading a multiagency effort to modify or eliminate federal regulations that may impose unnecessary collateral consequences on individuals with criminal records. • *Federal barriers to employment.* • An interagency working group identified critical opportunities for reducing federal barriers to employment. It developed an action plan that includes a broad set of strategies to promote model policies; enhance existing training, enforcement, and compliance monitoring authorities in this area; create public education materials; and increase companion services to help remove barriers to reentry. • The Secretary of Labor hosted a Roundtable on Workforce Development and Employment Strategies for people with criminal records. • The Equal Employment Opportunity Commission held a meeting examining private and government

Short-term goals	Accomplishments
	employers' use of arrest and conviction records in employment, the applicable legal standards, and best practices of employers. • The Equal Employment Opportunity Commission updated enforcement guidance on the use of arrest and conviction records in employment decisions. The revised guidance calls for employers to assess applicants on an individual basis rather than uniformly excluding those with criminal records from consideration. • The Department of Labor finalized and distributed guidance to the public workforce system regarding employer job postings that contain hiring exclusions/restrictions based on criminal history. • The Office of Personnel Management is considering revising federal hiring practices to ensure that individuals with criminal records are not unnecessarily deterred from pursuing federal job opportunities. • *Access to federal benefits and treatment.* • An interagency working group developed an action plan designed to improve access to federal benefits such as Temporary Assistance for Needy Families, food assistance, veterans, Social Security, and others that can help stabilize the reentry population, and by extension their families, after release. The action plan includes concrete coordination, training, and public education opportunities that will improve access by clarifying policies; increasing communications across agencies at the federal, regional, and state levels; and providing information and tools to direct service providers. • The Department of Veterans Affairs issued a policy change in April that expands eligibility for its health care to include individuals in community-based settings. • The Department of Veterans Affairs revised its administrative policy limiting its prison outreach to the 6 months prior to a veteran's release. The revised policy will allow assessment and release planning with incarcerated veterans to begin earlier, thus enhancing the odds of successful reentry and reintegration.

Table 9. (Continued)

Short-term goals	Accomplishments
	• The Department of Agriculture also surveyed its nationwide partners and their local affiliates to learn more about nutrition assistance services currently being provided and to build on promising practices in promoting benefit access to the reentry population. Department of Agriculture officials will research effective programs that collect information needed to apply prior to release, ensure that individuals have appropriate identification upon release, and conduct prerelease outreach on the Supplemental Nutritional Assistance Program, • The Social Security Administration is continuing to work with corrections officials to establish prerelease agreements for Social Security benefits and memorandums of understanding for replacement Social Security cards. • The Department of Health and Human Services is assisting the field in understanding how to improve access to health care and treatment for the returning population, including funding a pilot project with the Department of Justice's National Institute of Corrections to evaluate early access to Medicaid as a reentry strategy, and providing information about the Affordable Care Act and how its provisions might affect vulnerable populations, such as the reentry population. • *Child support issues for incarcerated parents.* As part of the Department of Health and Human Services, the Office of Child Support Enforcement is spearheading a subcommittee to identify child support barriers to reentry, to build new partnerships and enhance existing partnerships, and to coordinate and leverage resources for child support and reentry. • *Tax education products.* The Internal Revenue Service created new informational publications in English and Spanish that provide information on federal tax responsibilities, tax credits, and tax benefits and other information for the formerly incarcerated and consolidated this information on its designated Prisoner-Reentry Program webpage.

Short-term goals	Accomplishments
	Higher education policy. The Department of education engaged agency partners, internal stakeholders, and external advocacy groups to consider recent research on the now-widespread use of criminal background checks in the college admissions process.

Source: GAO analysis of Federal Interagency Reentry Council documents.
[a]United States Interagency Council on Homelessness, Searching Out Solutions: Constructive Alternatives to the Criminalization of Homelessness (Washington, D.C.: 2012).

APPENDIX III: SUMMARY OF ONGOING AGENCY REENTRY PROGRAM EVALUATIONS

Table 10 provides summary information about the Department of Justice and Department of Labor Second Chance Act (SCA) and Re-integration of Ex-offenders (RExO) evaluations of grant programs that support adult reentry services.[1]

Table 10. DOJ and Labor Reentry Grant Program Evaluations

Evaluation	Agency	Cost	Length	Description	Results Expected
SCA Evaluation of Honest Opportunity Probation with Enforcement Demonstration Field Experiment	DOJ National Institute of Justice	$2,499,944	42 months	Multisite evaluation to include a process evaluation to document the changes necessary to implement the program, an outcome evaluation to determine the program's impact on offender recidivism and probation compliance, and a costeffectiveness study to assess the programmatic costs and any potential savings achieved through reduced probation revocations.	March 2015

Table 10. (Continued)

Evaluation	Agency	Cost	Length	Description	Results Expected
SCA Reentry Court Evaluation	National Institute of Justice	$2,988,850	53 months	Multisite evaluation of the program to include a process evaluation to document and compare program models and implementation. An impact evaluation will examine rearrests, reconvictions, violations, and returns to incarceration using pre- and post-archival data and data from interviews and drug tests in select sites. Cost-benefit analyses will calculate avoided public costs by comparing program interventions with "business-as-usual" conditions.	Summer 2015
SCA Adult Demonstration Projects Evaluation	National Institute of Justice	$3,656,357	53 months	Evaluation of a subsample of 15 SCA adult demonstration sites funded by DOJ in 2009. The evaluation will include impact, process, and outcome analyses and cost assessments of reentry services provided by the sites.	Summer 2015 (interim results in spring 2013)[a]
SCA Adult Offender Reentry Demonstration Projects Evaluation	National Institute of Justice	$2,934,589	39 months	The evaluation will include a process, outcome, and cost evaluation of eight programs that were funded in fiscal years 2010 and 2011. The evaluation will study the programs to determine whether they achieved the primary goals of reducing recidivism and increasing public safety, as well as other goals, including increased employment and education opportunities, reduced violations of conditions of	Spring 2016

Evaluation	Agency	Cost	Length	Description	Results Expected
				release, increased payment of child support, increased housing opportunities, reduced drug and alcohol abuse, and increased access to substance abuse treatment and mental health services.	
SCA Evaluation of the Multisite Demonstration Field Experiment: What Works in Reentry Research	National Institute of Justice	$3,000,000	48 months	In an effort to provide rigorous evidence of what works in reentry, the National Institute of Justice will conduct one or more experiments of promising reentry interventions, strategies, or programs. Reentering offenders will be randomly assigned to receive the experimental treatment or to receive "business-asusual" reentry services (or some other clearly defined control treatment). The evaluation has been funded by the National Institute of Justice in partnership with the Bureau of Justice Assistance as part of the Demonstration Field Experiment program.	Winter 2016
Reintegration of Ex-Offenders Random Assignment Evaluation	Labor's Employment and Training Administration	$6,964,569	64 months	Random assignment evaluation of a demonstration serving formerly incarcerated individuals through employment-centered programs. The impact evaluation began in fiscal year 2008 and examines impacts on participants' postprogram labor market outcomes and rates of criminal recidivism by	June 2014

Table 10. DOJ and Labor Reentry Grant Program Evaluations

Evaluation	Agency	Cost	Length	Description	Results Expected
				comparing outcomes of RExO participants with the outcomes of randomly assigned individuals who are eligible for but do not receive RExO services.	

Source: GAO analysis of agency documents.

[a] This evaluation was originally scheduled to be completed in fall 2013. According to DOJ officials, the project was extended by 6 months to (1) allow for a 12-month post-treatment follow-up period for all SCA participants, and (2) allow grantees time to collect criminal history and administrative data for all offenders who received SCA services if the offenders' informed consent has been secured. These data will be used to create recidivism rates for the sample.

End Notes

[1] For data on the number of individuals incarcerated, see Department of Justice, Bureau of Justice Statistics, Correctional Populations in the United States, 2011 (Washington, D.C.: November 2012). Bureau of Justice Statistics' data on correctional expenditures are preliminary. The Bureau of Justice Statistics is the statistical agency of Department of Justice.

[2] U.S. Department of Justice, Office of Justice Programs, Bureau of Justice Statistics, Special Report: Recidivism of Prisoners Released in 1994, (Washington, D.C.: June 2002). According to Department of Justice officials, the Bureau of Justice Assistance is currently working on a new national recidivism study that involved about 30 states and 75,000 former inmates. DOJ estimates that the report will be completed by December 31, 2012.

[3] GAO, Bureau of Prisons: Growing Inmate Crowding Negatively Affects Inmates, Staff, and Infrastructure, GAO-12-743 (Washington, D.C.: Sept. 12, 2012).

[4] Agencies included on the Federal Interagency Reentry Council and the council's working group are the Department of Justice, Department of the Interior, Department of Agriculture, Department of Labor, Department of Health and Human Services, Department of Housing and Urban Development, Department of Education, Department of Veterans Affairs, Office of National Drug Control Policy, Social Security Administration, Domestic Policy Council, Equal Employment Opportunity Commission, White House Office of Faith-Based and Neighborhood Partnerships, Office of Personnel Management, Office of Management and Budget, Internal Revenue Service, Federal Trade Commission, Interagency Council on Homelessness, Small Business Administration, and Court Services and Offender Supervision Agency—the last of which is only on the Federal Interagency Reentry Council's working group. Collateral costs quantify the size of the effect of incarceration to both the individual and the individual's family.

[5] The Federal Interagency Reentry Council has no separate budget, and council representatives participate in council activities while also fulfilling their respective responsibilities at their home agencies. In contrast, the United States Interagency Council on Homelessness receives a separate appropriation from Congress and employs full-time staff.

[6] The SCA program is carried out through the authority provided in the Second Chance Act of 2007, Pub. L. No. 110-199, 122 Stat. 657 (2008). The RExO program is carried out through authority provided in Section 171 of the Workforce Investment Act of 1998, Pub. L. No. 105-220, 112 Stat. 936, 1031-34, and Section 212 of the Second Chance Act of 2007, Pub. L. No. 110-199, 122 Stat. 657, 680-83. HHS's ORP grants are authorized under Section 509 of the Public Health Service Act, as amended.

[7] GAO, Federal Grants: Improvements Needed in Oversight and Accountability Processes, GAO-11-773T (Washington, D.C.: June 23, 2011).

[8] GAO, Opportunities to Reduce Potential Duplication in Government Programs, Save Tax Dollars, and Enhance Revenue, GAO-11-318SP (Washington, D.C.: Mar. 1, 2011), and 2012 Annual Report: Opportunities to Reduce Duplication, Overlap and Fragmentation, Achieve Savings, and Enhance Revenue, GAO-12-342SP (Washington, D.C.: Feb. 28, 2012).

[9] GAO, Justice Grant Programs: DOJ Should Do More to Reduce the Risk of Unnecessary Duplication and Enhance Program Assessment, GAO-12-517 (Washington, D.C.: July 12, 2012).

[10] The actions we suggested that would help address this issue are discussed later in this report, along with the agency's position.

[11] CFDA is a government-wide compendium of federal programs, projects, services, and activities that provide assistance or benefits to the American public. Grants.gov serves as the central grant identification and application portal for more than 1,000 federal grant programs. USAspending.gov displays data pertaining to federal grants.

[12] GAO-11-318SP and GAO-12-342SP.

[13] The Council of State Governments Justice Center is a national nonprofit organization that serves policymakers at the local, state, and federal levels from all branches of government. We spoke to officials on the Association of State Correctional Administrators Reentry and Community Corrections Committee, which works to identify and implement best practices in reentry and community-based programs to reduce the number of inmates returning to prison after release. We met with these organizations because of their experience with the reentry field.

[14] Specifically, we met with officials from DOJ's Office of Justice Programs, including the Bureau of Justice Assistance; Office of Audit, Assessment, and Management; and National Institute of Justice; DOJ's BOP, including the National Institute of Corrections; Labor's Employment and Training Administrations and Office of Grants Management; and HHS's Administration for Children and Families, National Institutes of Health, Assistant Secretary for Planning and Evaluation; and Substance Abuse and Mental Health Services Administration.

[15] GAO, Results-Oriented Government: Practices That Can Help Enhance and Sustain Collaboration among Federal Agencies, GAO-06-15 (Washington, D.C.: Oct. 21, 2005).

[16] Pub. L. No. 111-352, 124 Stat. 3866 (2011). The GPRA Modernization Act amends the Government Performance and Results Act of 1993, Pub. L. No. 103-62, 107 Stat. 285 (1993).

[17] Federal Bureau of Prisons FY 2013 Budget Request, Before the Committee on Appropriations, Subcommittee of Commerce, Justice, Science and Related Agencies, 112th Cong. 203 (2012) (statement of Charles E. Samuels, Jr., Director of the Federal Bureau of Prisons).

[18] Urban Institute, Life After Prison: Tracking the Experiences of Male Prisoners Returning to Chicago, Cleveland, and Houston (Washington, D.C.: May 2010), and One Year Out: Tracking the Experiences of Male Prisoners Returning to Houston, Texas, (Washington, D.C.: June 2009).

[19] In September 2012, DOJ's National Institute of Justice established a public website to inventory state and federal legal and regulatory sanctions and restrictions that result in collateral consequences of conviction.

[20] According to various research, as well as federal officials, reentry programs are essential for those former inmates who are at a high risk for recidivism; however, research on low-risk offenders shows that it can be detrimental to their reentry success to provide too much intervention.

[21] Both programs were implemented under the authority granted by the reentry program codified at 42 U.S.C. § 3797w.

[22] Pub. L. No. 110-199, 122 Stat. 657 (2008).

[23] Specifically, in fiscal year 2011, DOJ issued eight solicitations that provided funding for direct services for the adult reentry population under the SCA program: (1) Adult Mentoring Grants to Non-Profit Organizations; (2) Adult Offender Reentry Program for Planning and Demonstration Projects; (3) State, Local, and Tribal Reentry Courts; (4) Adult Offenders with Co-occurring Substance Abuse and Mental Health Disorders; (5) A Family-Based Offender Substance Abuse Treatment Program; (6) Technology Careers Training Demonstration Projects for Incarcerated Adults and Juveniles; (7) The Honest Opportunity Probation with Enforcement Demonstration Field Experiment; and (8) Demonstration Field Experiment: Fostering Desistance Through Effective Supervision.

[24] Pub. L. No. 105-220, 112 Stat. 936.

[25] 42 U.S.C. § 290bb-2.

[26] Pub. L. No. 111-139, § 21, 124 Stat. 8, 29-30 (2010).

[27] GAO-11-318SP and GAO-12-342SP.

[28] GAO-12-517 and GAO-12-342SP.

[29] GAO-12-517.

[30] This amount includes funding for "new" awards—awards for grantees that are not currently receiving funds, and does not include funding for "continuation" awards—awards made to grantees to continue a program that was initially awarded funding in a prior year. Some of the grant solicitations that awarded funds in fiscal year 2011 were open to both juvenile and adult reentry populations.

[31] Indigent defense refers to the defense of individuals accused of a crime and unable to afford representation.

[32] 42 U.S.C. § 3797w.

[33] 42 U.S.C. § 290bb-2.

[34] Included in the five grant programs that were open to all categories of applicants is the SCA grant program; however, only one of the eight solicitations for that program in fiscal year 2011 was open to nonprofit organizations. This solicitation required grant applicants to partner with a governmental agency.

[35] GAO, Science, Technology, Engineering, and Mathematics Education: Strategic Planning Needed to Better Manage Overlapping Programs across Multiple Agencies, GAO-12-108 (Washington, D.C.: Jan. 20, 2012); Homelessness: Fragmentation and Overlap in Programs

Highlight the Need to Identify, Assess, and Reduce Inefficiencies, GAO-12-491(Washington, D.C.: May 10, 2012); and Financial Literacy: Overlap of Programs Suggests There May Be Opportunities for Consolidation, GAO-12-588 (Washington, D.C.: July 23, 2012).

[36] Data for the SCA and ORP program are from 2011, and data for the RExO program are from 2010—the most recent annual data available.

[37] GAO-12-517.

[38] GAO-06-15.

[39] Pub. L. No. 110-199, § 101, 122 Stat. 657, 666-667 (2008) (codified at 42 U.S.C. § 3797w).

[40] The National Reentry Resource Center is funded by the Bureau of Justice Assistance, DOJ; the Public Welfare Foundation; the Annie E. Casey Foundation; the Open Society Institute; and the Joyce Foundation.

[41] GAO-12-517.

[42] GAO-12-517.

[43] Additionally, DOJ reported in September 2012 that all fiscal year 2012 solicitations issued through its Office of Justice Programs now include a clause that grantees must report to DOJ any federal funds they receive that have been, are being, or will be used, in whole or in part, for one or more of the identical cost items for which the Office of Justice Programs granted them funds for already.

[44] Under the Second Chance Act of 2007, Pub. L. No. 110-199, § 101, 122 Stat. 657, 664- 667 (2008) (codified at 42 U.S.C. § 3797w), grantees are required to measure their progress toward increasing public safety by reducing rates of recidivism.

[45] The Bureau of Justice Statistics conducted two studies of recidivism of released prisoners that provide national estimates of the recidivism rate of prisoners in the 1980s and 1990s.

[46] Department of Justice, Office of Justice Programs, Bureau of Justice Statistics, Recidivism of Prisoners Released in 1994 (Washington, D.C.: 2002), and Recidivism of Prisoners Released in 1983 (Washington, D.C.: 1989).

[47] Bureau of Justice Statistics, Recidivism of Prisoners Released in 1994.

[48] GAO, Bureau of Prisons, Improved Evaluations and Increased Coordination Could Improve Cell Phone Detection, GAO-11-893 (Washington, D.C.: Sept. 6, 2011), and GAO-06-15.

[49] GAO, Managing for Results: A Guide for Using the GPRA Modernization Act to Help Inform Congressional Decision Making, GAO-12-621SP (Washington, D.C.: June 15, 2012), and Agencies' Annual Performance Plans under the Results Act: An Assessment Guide to Facilitate Congressional Decisionmaking, GAO/GGD/AIMD-10.1.18 (Washington, D.C.: Feb. 1, 1998).

[50] GAO, Performance Measurement and Evaluation, Definitions and Relationships, GAO-11-646SP (Washington, D.C.: May 2, 2011), and Program Evaluation, Studies Helped Agencies Measure or Explain Program Performance, GAO/GGD-00-204 (Washington, D.C.: Sept. 29, 2000).

[51] Pub. L. No. 110-199, § 101, 122 Stat. 657, 667 (2008) (codified at 42 U.S.C. § 3797w(n)).

[52] Evaluation of the Prisoner Re-Entry Initiative. A report prepared at the request of the Department of Labor, Jan.13, 2009.

[53] Pamela K. Lattimore and Christy A. Visher, The Multi-site Evaluation of SVORI: Summary and Synthesis. A report prepared at the request of the Department of Justice, December 2009.

[54] Pamela K. Lattimore and Christy A. Visher, et al. Prisoner Reentry Services: What Worked for SVORI Evaluation Participants? (Washington, D.C.: Feb. 2012). The Department of Justice provided federal funds for this report to be prepared.

[55] DOJ Office of the Inspector General, Office of Justice Programs' Management of Its Offender Reentry Initiatives (Washington, D.C.: July 2010).

[56] HHS Office of the Inspector General, Top Management and Performance Challenges Facing the Department of Health and Human *Services in Fiscal Year 2011*, (Washington, D.C.: November 2011).

End Notes for Appendix I

[1] GAO, Bureau of Prisons: Growing Inmate Crowding Negatively Affects Inmates, Staff, and Infrastructure, GAO-12-743 (Washington, D.C.: Sept. 12, 2012).

[2] GAO, Federal Bureau of Prisons: BOP Has Mechanisms in Place to Address Most Second Chance Act Requirements and Is Working to Implement an Initiative Designed to Reduce Recidivism, GAO-10-854R (Washington, D.C.: July 14, 2010).

End Note for Appendix II

[1] Agencies include the Department of Justice, Department of Interior, Department of Agriculture, Department of Labor, Department of Health and Human Services, Department of Housing and Urban Development, Department of Education, Department of Veterans Affairs, Office of National Drug Control Policy, Social Security Administration, Domestic Policy Council, Equal Employment Opportunity Commission, White House Office of Faith-Based and Neighborhood Partnerships, Office of Personnel Management, Office of Management and Budget, Internal Revenue Service, Federal Trade Commission, Interagency Council on Homelessness, Small Business Administration, and Court Services and Offender Supervision Agency.

End Note for Appendix III

[1] There are multiple forms of evaluation studies including (1) process or implementation evaluation, which assesses the extent to which a program is operating as it was intended. It typically assesses program activities' conformance to statutory and regulatory requirements, program design, and professional standards or customer expectations; (2) outcome evaluation, which assesses the extent to which a program achieves its outcome-oriented objectives. It focuses on outputs and outcomes (including unintended effects) to judge program effectiveness but may also assess program process to understand how outcomes are produced; (3) impact evaluation, which is a form of outcome evaluation that assesses the net effect of a program by comparing program outcomes with an estimate of what would have happened in the absence of the program. This form of evaluation is employed when external factors are known to influence the program's outcomes, in order to isolate the program's contribution to achievement of its objectives; (4) cost-benefit and cost-effectiveness analysis, which are analyses that compare a program's outputs or outcomes with the costs (resources expended) to produce them. When applied to existing programs, they are also

considered a form of program evaluation. Cost-effectiveness analysis assesses the cost of meeting a single goal or objective and can be used to identify the least costly alternative for meeting that goal. Cost-benefit analysis aims to identify all relevant costs and benefits, usually expressed in dollar terms.

INDEX

C

D

H

I

J

L

M

N

O

P

R

S

W